INTRODUCTION

Beginning Bridge Complete was written to provide bridge students and teachers with a functional Standard American text based on five-card majors. Unlike many other books, it is suitable for self-teaching or for classroom use. The format is simple: you start at the beginning, learn the mechanics of the game, and continue with an in-depth examination of bidding and play. A self-testing quiz is included at the end of each chapter, and a thorough glossary, of great help to beginners, is found at the end of the book. Even if you have never played bridge before, *Beginning Bridge Complete* will have you playing and enjoying bridge before you know it.

Good luck!

—Mike Lawrence

D0401219

Chapter 1
MECHANICS

Bridge is played by four persons using a standard deck of 52 playing cards. The deck is divided into four suits—spades, hearts, diamonds, and clubs. Spades and hearts are called *major suits*. Diamonds and clubs are called *minor suits*. There are 13 cards in each suit, ranking from highest to lowest as follows: Ace, King, Queen, Jack, 10, 9, 8, 7, 6, 5, 4, 3, 2. The Ace, King, Queen, Jack and 10 are referred to as honor cards, or *honors*.

To start the game, partnerships are agreed upon and the players are seated opposite their respective partners. The following illustrates a common arrangement at the outset of a bridge game:

North and South are partners versus East and West. Assume South is to deal the first hand. South shuffles the cards and presents them to East to be cut. After the cards are cut, South deals the cards one at a time face down in clockwise rotation. The first card goes to West, the second card to North, and so on around the table until all the cards have been dealt. The four players then pick up their cards (13 each) and sort them into suits. The dealer bids first, and the bidding proceeds in clockwise rotation until it is concluded. If all four players pass, the cards are thrown in and redealt.

After all the cards have been dealt, each player will have 13 cards. Your cards (called your hand) might look something like this:

♠ A J 7 5 2
♡ K 5 4 3
♢ Q 10 9
♣ 6

BEGINNING BRIDGE COMPLETE

by Michael Penick

Published by
Devyn Press
Louisville, Kentucky

Cover by Bonnie Baron Pollack
Illustrations by Jude Goodwin

Devyn Press, Inc.
3600 Chamberlain Lane, Suite 230
Louisville, KY 40241
1-800-274-2221

Seventh Printing - 2003
ISBN 0-910791-06-6

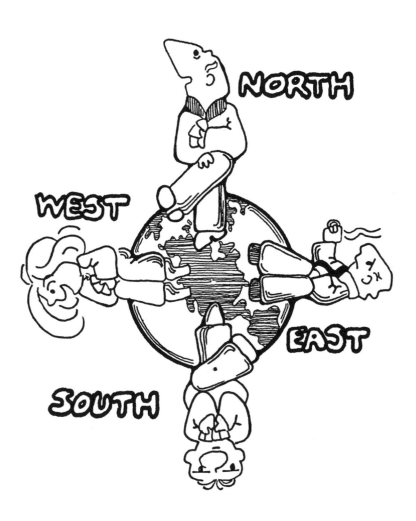

WHAT NEXT?

Now that you have your cards sorted into suits, you next determine whether you have a good hand or a bad hand. This is done by *evaluating* your hand. You evaluate in the following manner:

For each Ace . . . . count 4 points
For each King . . . . count 3 points
For each Queen . . . . count 2 points
For each Jack . . . . count 1 point

Points which you count in evaluating your hand as outlined above, that is, points assigned to Aces, Kings, Queens, and Jacks, are called *high-card points (HCPs)*. For example, the hand below contains ten high-card points:

♠ A 5 4 3 2
♡ K 10 5 4
◊ Q J 3
♣ 8

The high-card point value of the above hand is 10 points, but is that the entire value of the hand? The answer is no. After you have counted the high-card points in your hand, you must next count *distributional points*.

Distributional points are points which you add to the value of your hand for shortness in a suit. If you have no cards in a suit (called a *void*), you add three points to the value of your hand. If you have only one card in a suit (called a *singleton*), you add two points to the value of your hand. If you have only two cards in a suit (called a *doubleton*), add one point to the value of your hand. The total of high-card points and distributional points gives you the total value of your hand.

You will recall that in the sample hand above you counted your high-card points and came up with a total of 10. To complete the evaluation of that hand, you must also check for short suits in order to assess and add your distributional points to the value of your hand. In checking the sample hand, you note that

you have a singleton club. You therefore add two points to the high-card total of 10 and arrive at a total of 12 points. This is the total value of your hand.

The following charts will assist you in evaluating bridge hands.

POINT COUNT EVALUATION

High-Card Points

Each Ace.................4 points
Each King................3 points
Each Queen ....2 points
Each Jack................1 point

Distributional Points

Each Void................3 points
Each Singleton ....2 points
Each Doubleton ....1 point

NOTE: If you have a singleton King, Queen or Jack, count only one distributional point for that singleton; in other words, this singleton will be worth one point less than a singleton is usually counted. Thus, a singleton King is evaluated as four points (three points for the high-card value of the King plus one point for the revised value of the singleton); a singleton Queen is evaluated as three points; and a singleton Jack is evaluated as two points. For example:

♠ A 9 7 5
♡ K 5 4 2
◊ J
♣ K 5 4 3

    In counting the high-card points in this hand, the Ace of spades equals four points, the King of hearts equals three points, the Jack of diamonds equals one point, and the King of clubs equals three points. Therefore, the hand contains 11 HCPs.

    Next count the distributional points. The singleton diamond would normally be evaluated at two points. However, in this case the singleton is a Jack, so add only one point for distribution.

    The total value of the hand is 11 HCPs plus one distributional point, a total of 12 points.

If you have a doubleton Queen or Jack, count no distributional point for that doubleton. In other words, a doubleton Queen is worth a total of two points and a doubleton Jack is worth a total of 1 point. Doubleton Aces and Kings are worth their normal values.

    After everyone has had an opportunity to sort his cards into suits and count his points, each player will know the initial value of his hand. At this point, the bidding may commence.

WHO BIDS FIRST?

    The dealer bids first. The dealer may either bid a suit or may pass. As we said earlier, if all four players pass, the hand is thrown in and a new hand is dealt. However, one of the players will usually *open the bidding*. For example, the bidding may be opened 1♣, 1♠, 2♡, etc. You should open the bidding if the value of your hand totals 13 or more points, combining high-card points and distributional points. Assuming someone does in fact open the bidding, the bidding proceeds clockwise until there are three consecutive passes. When three consecutive passes have occurred, the bidding is over and the play of the hand is ready to begin.

NOW WHAT?

We used the abbreviations N-S and E-W to designate the partnerships in the diagram on page 4. This is the common method of designating places around a bridge table, the letters designating North, South, East, and West. A sample bidding sequence is shown below:

NORTH	EAST	SOUTH	WEST
Pass	Pass	1 ♠	Pass
2 ♠	Pass	Pass	Pass

In the diagram above, North is the dealer and is therefore the first person to speak. The bidding then proceeds clockwise and South opens the bidding with 1 ♠. West passes and North bids 2 ♠. Thereafter, there are three consecutive passes which, as we know, mean the bidding is over. The final *contract* is 2 ♠.

We must next determine who is to be the *declarer*. The declarer is the person who is to play the hand. The declarer in the above example is South, because South was the first person to bid the suit that became the final contract. In the example above, the contract is 2 ♠ and the declarer is South.

THE PLAY

The play of a bridge hand is a very simple process. You first determine the declarer. The person to the left of the declarer plays one card to the center of the table. The declarer's partner then becomes the *dummy* and lays his cards face up on the table, opposite the declarer. The declarer's partner (the dummy) makes no further play of any kind during that hand. Rather, his cards are played by his partner, the declarer. In the example above, South is the declarer. West, therefore, plays a card to the center of the table, after which North lays his cards face up on the table arranged in suits with the trump suit on his right. South plays one of North's cards to the center of the table. East then plays a card and finally South plays a card from his hand to the center of the table. These four cards, one played by each person, constitute a *trick*. The player winning the first trick leads the first card to the second trick. All players play in clockwise rotation, one card to each trick, and play continues until all 13 tricks have been played. At this point, the hand is concluded.

OBJECT OF THE GAME

The object of the game is to win as many tricks as possible. After the bidding has concluded and the declarer is ready to play the hand, the person to his left may lead any card of any of the four suits. This is called the *opening lead.* Each player must follow suit, if possible. The highest card of the suit that was originally led wins that trick.

TRUMPS

Normally bridge hands are played with some suit designated as a *trump* suit. In the example hand shown previously, the final contract was 2♠, making spades the trump suit.

POWER OF THE TRUMP SUIT

Assume that 2♠ is the final contract and that spades are trumps. Assume that the opening lead is the Ace of diamonds. You know that if you have a diamond, you must play a diamond, and that the Ace will win the trick. However, if any player does not have a diamond, he may, if he chooses, trump the trick by playing a spade. The power of the trump will override the power of the Ace of diamonds, and the player trumping the trick will win that trick.

HOW MANY TRICKS MUST BE WON?

The answer to this query depends upon what the contract is and whether your side is declaring or defending. Assume the contract is 2♠ and that your side is declaring. You will remember that there are 13 possible tricks to be won in each hand. In order to make 2♠, you must win eight tricks. Why eight? Because the rules of bridge require that the declaring side *make book.* Make book merely means that the side who gets the contract must win six tricks before that side can begin counting tricks toward its contract. Therefore, if the contract is 2♠, the declaring side must take six tricks (book), plus two additional tricks. The number of tricks required to make any bid is six plus the number bid. Some examples will make this clear:

THE BOOK

Example 1: Contract—4 hearts
Declarer must win 10 tricks to make his contract (6 + 4)

Example 2: Contract—1 diamond
Declarer must win 7 tricks to make his contract (6 + 1)

Example 3: Contract—5 clubs
Declarer must win 11 tricks to make his contract (6 + 5)

The goal of the defending side is, of course, to prevent the declarer from making the number of tricks required for his contract. For example, if the contract is 3 ◊, we know that declarer requires nine tricks to make his contract. The defenders, therefore, set their goal at winning five tricks, because if they take five tricks, the declarer will have taken only eight and will have failed to make his contract.

HOW HIGH CAN I BID?

The astute reader will have realized that the highest level to which one can bid in bridge is the seven level. Since the declarer must take six tricks for book before he can start counting tricks toward his contract, and since there are only 13 possible tricks, it is obvious that a bid at the seven level requires the declaring side to make all 13 tricks.

RANK OF SUITS

There are four suits in bridge that we already know about: spades, hearts, diamonds and clubs. In addition, there is a fifth denomination called *notrump*. Notrump means no suit is trump. If the final contract is in spades, hearts, diamonds or clubs, the suit last bid is the trump suit; if notrump is the final bid, then nothing is trump during that hand.

The chart below indicates the rank of notrump and the suits:

RANKING:
Notrump
Spades
Hearts
Diamonds
Clubs

From the chart, we see that notrump has the highest rank, followed by spades, hearts, and diamonds, with clubs having the lowest rank.

EFFECT OF THE RANK OF SUITS ON BIDDING

The rank of suits is very important in the bidding. The reason is that suits of a higher rank may be bid at the same level over suits of a lower rank. For example, if the player to your right deals and opens the bidding 1 ♣, you may bid 1 ◊, 1 ♡, 1 ♠ or 1 notrump as you wish. However, if the player to your right opens the bidding 1 ♠ and you wish to bid clubs, diamonds, or hearts, you must bid your suit at the two level. The reason is that clubs, diamonds, and hearts are lower-ranking suits than spades.

The foregoing constitutes the basic mechanics of the game of bridge. To understand them and to understand all of the material in this book, I strongly urge you to practice each phase of the game as you learn it.

"But I don't know how to play!" you protest.

You already know more than you think. You can deal a bridge hand, arrange your cards into suits, count your points, and arrive at the correct total. If you cannot, review this chapter, then check your progress by answering the questions found in Quiz No. 1.

QUIZ NO. 1

1. You hold:　♠ A Q 10 4
　　　　　　　♡ K 5 3
　　　　　　　◊ J 9 7
　　　　　　　♣ Q J 2

How many high-card points do you hold?　＿＿＿＿＿＿

How many distributional points do you hold?＿＿＿＿＿

What is the total value of this hand?　＿＿＿＿＿＿＿

2. You hold: ♠ 9 8 5
              ♡ A K 5 3 2
              ◊ 5
              ♣ Q J 6 3

How many high-card points do you hold? _____

How many distributional points do you hold? _____

What is the total value of this hand? _____

3. You hold: ♠ K J 9 8 7 6
              ♡ A Q J 5
              ◊ 9 8
              ♣ 4

How many high-card points do you hold? _____

How many distributional points do you hold? _____

What is the total value of this hand? _____

4. You hold: ♠ Q
              ♡ A K Q 9 8 6
              ◊ J 10 5 2
              ♣ 4 2

How many high-card points do you hold? _____

How many distributional points do you hold? _____

What is the total value of this hand? _____

5. You hold: ♠ Q 5 2
              ♡ K J 4 3
              ◊ A 9 8 7
              ♣ 5 4

How many high-card points do you hold? _____

How many distributional points do you hold? _____

What is the total value of this hand? _____

6. Each player is dealt _____ cards at the beginning of each bridge hand. The _____ bids first.

7. The person playing the final contract is called the
_____.

8. The person to the declarer's _____ makes the opening lead. The declarer then plays a card from dummy, after which the person to the declarer's _____plays a card. Finally, the declarer plays a card. These four cards comprise one _____ .

9. There are _____ tricks in each hand of bridge.

10. There are _____ denominations (suits + notrump) in bridge. They rank from highest to lowest as follows:

_____
_____
_____
_____
_____

11. What are honors? _____

NOTE: The answers to each quiz follow on the next page after the quiz. For your own benefit, take the quiz to see what you need to study before turning to the answers. In other words, NO PEEKING!

ANSWERS TO QUIZ NO. 1

1. high-card points 13
   distributional points 0
   total points 13

2. high-card points 10
   distributional points 2
   total points 12

3. high-card points 11
   distributional points 3
   total points 14

4. high-card points 12
   distributional points 2
   (We count only one distributional point for the singleton because the singleton is a Queen.)
   total points 14

5. high-card points 10
   distributional points 1
   total points 11

6. 13; dealer

7. declarer

8. left; right; trick

9. 13

10. 5; notrump, spades, hearts, diamonds, clubs

11. Ace, King, Queen, Jack, and 10

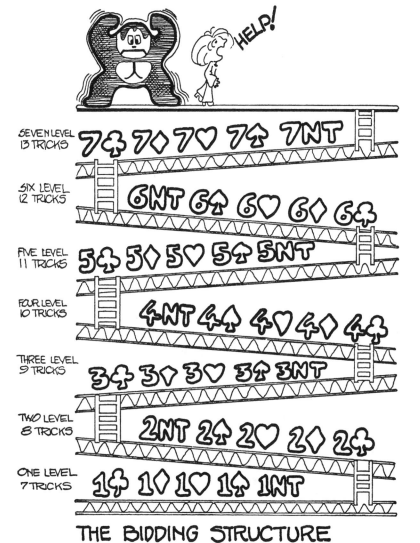

THE BIDDING STRUCTURE

Chapter 2
SCORING

At the outset of a bridge game someone is designated to keep score. The customary method of keeping score is to draw a cross on a piece of paper and designate the teams as "WE" and "THEY". At the beginning of a bridge contest, before either side has scored, the score sheet should look like this:

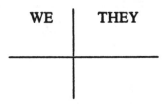

Note the horizontal line dividing the page. That line is present for a particular purpose. Points scored for tricks bid and made toward game are entered below the horizontal line. All other scores are entered above the line.

We shall first discuss points scored by the declaring side, assuming that the declaring side has bid and made a contract.

You will recall that a contract of 2♠ (or 2 of anything else, for that matter) requires that the declaring side take eight tricks. The first six tricks won by the declarer constitute book. Each trick bid and made over book is counted toward the contract. Thus, as indicated above, eight tricks must be made by the declaring side in order to successfully make a contract of 2♠. Should you make your contract, you will score points for your side; similarly, should you fail to make your contract, your opponents will score.

HOW MANY POINTS WILL I SCORE?

For each trick bid and made above book in clubs and diamonds, the declaring side scores 20 points. For each trick bid and made above book in hearts or spades, the declaring side scores 30 points. Should you play and make a notrump contract, you score 40 points for the first trick bid and made above book and 30 points for each additional trick bid and made.

700

100

100

Example 1:   1♣ bid and made — score 20 points.
Example 2:   2♡ bid and made — score 60 points.
Example 3:   1 Notrump bid and made — score 40 points.
Example 4:   3 Notrump bid and made — score 100 points.

In order to make a game, you must score 100 points. You may score these 100 points in only one hand or in a combination of hands. For example, if you bid 3 Notrump and take nine tricks, you will score 100 points, that being 40 points for the first notrump trick and 30 points for each additional trick (40 + 30 + 30 = 100 points). Therefore, you have bid and made game in one hand. Similarly, since hearts and spades count 30 points per trick, you must bid and make 4♡ or 4♠ in order to score game in one hand (30 × 4 = 120 points). Since clubs and diamonds count only 20 points per trick, you must bid and make 5♣ or 5♢ in order to score game in one hand (20 × 5 = 100 points).

On some hands, you will not have sufficient strength to bid game. If you play a contract below game, that contract is called a *part score* or *partial*.

If you succeed in making more than one part score, you may add your part score results together, and if they total 100 or more points, you have achieved game. For example, assume that on the first hand dealt, you bid and make 2♢ for a score of 40 points. Since you are the scorekeeper, you enter the 40 points on your score sheet, making the sheet look like this:

WE	THEY
40	

On the next hand, your opponents bid and make 3♠. This scores 90 points and you enter that on the score sheet on the opponents' side of the ledger. The score sheet now looks like this:

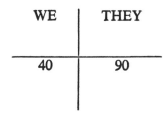

	WE	THEY
	40	90

On the third hand, assume that you bid and make a contract of 2 Notrump. You score 40 points for the first notrump and 30 for the second for a total of 70 points. These points also count toward game and you enter them on the score sheet. You will note that you have now scored 110 points, or 10 more than needed for game. You have therefore won a game and you indicate that on the score sheet by drawing a line and putting an arrow toward your side. The score sheet now:

	WE	THEY
	40	90
	70	

You now deal the fourth hand and your opponents bid and make 2♡. They score 60 points, which is entered below the line on the score sheet:

	WE	THEY
	40	90
	70	
		60

Have the opponents now made a game? The answer is no. Once one side or the other scores a game, all part scores previously achieved no longer count toward game. Your opponents now have a 60 part score and still must score 40 points below the line in order to win a game.

THE CONCEPT OF VULNERABILITY

Continuing our sample bridge game, you know that you have now won a game. In bridge, you like to win as many games as possible, but when you have won a game, your side becomes *vulnerable*. Being vulnerable means that your side is exposed to greater penalties for failing to make any subsequent contract it may bid. Exactly how these points are increased will be discussed later; for now it is important only to know that winning a game makes your side vulnerable.

RUBBERS AND OVERTRICKS

Bridge is scored in *rubbers*. In order to win a rubber, one side must win two out of three games. One side may win the first two games or may win the rubber by a score of two games to one.

Should you and partner win a rubber by winning the first two games, you will score a bonus of 700 points. If you win the rubber by two games to one, you score a bonus of 500 points. These points are scored above the line.

Tricks scored by the declaring side in excess of the number required in order to make a particular bid are called *overtricks*. Assume that you have bid a contract of 2♠ and that you are the declarer. You win nine tricks. You have obviously made your bid, which required only eight tricks. However, you scored nine tricks, which means that you have scored one overtrick. In scoring this hand, you will credit your side with 60 points below the line toward game and 30 points above the line for the extra trick which you made. Points scored above the line do not count toward making a game.

SLAM BONUSES

You may contract for a small slam by bidding at the six level. You must take 12 tricks to achieve this contract. You may also bid a grand slam, which requires you to take all 13 tricks.* Should you bid and make a small slam or grand slam, you score a bonus as follows:

> Small slam, not vulnerable .... 500 points
> Small slam, vulnerable .... 750 points
> Grand slam, not vulnerable ...... 1000 points
> Grand slam, vulnerable .... 1500 points

HONORS

Sometimes you will be dealt a large number of honors in one hand. In a suit contract, you score a bonus of 100 points if you hold four of the five honors in the trump suit in your hand. If you hold all five of the top honors, your bonus is 150. These points are scored above the line.

When the contract is played in notrump, the honors for purposes of assessing bonus points are the four Aces. If all four Aces are in one hand, a score of 150 points is credited above the line. It does not matter whether the person holding the honors is a member of the declaring side or the defending side—all that is necessary to score honors is to claim them at the end of the hand.

SCORING BY THE DEFENDERS

The only way in which the defenders can score points is to set the contract. Exactly how many points the defenders score depends on how many tricks the contract goes down, whether the declaring side was vulnerable or not vulnerable, and whether the contract was undoubled, doubled, or redoubled.*

---

*We will learn more about these terms in later chapters. If you would like a further explanation at this time, see **small slam, grand slam, double,** and **redouble** in the glossary.

REVIEW QUIZ #1

WHAT IS WRONG WITH THIS PICTURE?

ANSWER: THERE ARE ONLY THREE PEOPLE—IT TAKES FOUR TO PLAY BRIDGE

For each undoubled undertrick the defenders score 50 points if the opponents are not vulnerable, or 100 points if the opponents are vulnerable.

If the opponents are not vulnerable and the contract is doubled, the first undertrick is worth 100 points, the second and third undertricks are each worth 200 more, and each subsequent undertrick is worth 300 more.

If the opponents are vulnerable and the contract is doubled, the first undertrick is worth 200 points and each subsequent undertrick is worth 300 more.

All of the points for defeating a contract are scored above the line. The number of points scored by the defending side for any given contract is set out in the chart on page 28.

SCORING CHART

Contracts bid and made	Points
Clubs	20 points for each trick, scored below the line
Diamonds	20 points for each trick, scored below the line
Hearts	30 points for each trick, scored below the line
Spades	30 points for each trick, scored below the line
Notrump	40 points for the first trick, and 30 points for each succeeding trick, scored below the line

Score required for game	100 points
Bonuses for rubbers: if first two games won	700 points
if two out of three games won	500 points
Small slam not vulnerable	500 points
vulnerable	750 points

Grand slam	
not vulnerable	1000 points
vulnerable	1500 points

Bonuses for making
doubled contracts

A. Double your bid score below the line

B. 50 points bonus + 100 points for each overtrick if not vulnerable and 200 points for each overtrick if vulnerable, scored above the line

Bonuses for making
redoubled contracts

A. Quadruple your bid score below the line

B. 50 Points bonus + twice the doubled score for each overtrick

PREMIUMS FOR DEFEATING CONTRACTS

Down	Not Vul. Undoubled	Not Vul. Doubled	Vul. Undoubled	Vul. Doubled
1	50	100	100	200
2	100	300	200	500
3	150	500	300	800
4	200	800	400	1100
5	250	1100	500	1400
6	300	1400	600	1700
7	350	1700	700	2000
8	400	2000	800	2300
9	450	2300	900	2600
10	500	2600	1000	2900
11	550	2900	1100	3200
12	600	3200	1200	3500
13	650	3500	1300	3800

NOTE: To compute the score for going down redoubled, simply find the appropriate result for a doubled contract in the chart above and multiply it by two.

When the session of bridge is complete, add up *all* points for each side scored both above and below the line. The side with the most total points is the winner.

Now check your scorekeeping ability by answering the questions in Quiz No. 2.

QUIZ NO. 2

1. Draw a typical score sheet.

2. How many points does the declaring side score for bidding and making 1 ♣ or 1 ◇? _____

3. How many points does the declaring side score for bidding and making 1 ♡ or 1 ♠? _____

4. Should you bid and make a notrump contract, you score how many points for the first trick made above book?
   _____

   How many points for each additional trick bid and made?
   _____

5. How many points are necessary for game? _____

6. If you play a contract below game, that contract is called a
   _____.

7. How do you indicate that a side has won a game on the score sheet?

8. The side that has won a game is later exposed to greater penalties for failing to make any subsequent contracts. That side is now _____.

9. How many games must be won in order to win a rubber?
   _____

10. If you win the first two games, you will score a bonus of
    _____ points. If you win two out of three games, you will score a bonus of _____ points.

11. Tricks scored by the declaring side in excess of the number required in order to make that particular bid are called _____.

12. What are the bonus points for making:
    small slam, vulnerable   _____
    small slam, not vulnerable   _____
    grand slam, vulnerable   _____
    grand slam, not vulnerable   _____

13. If you should hold four of the five trump honors in your hand, you will receive a bonus of _____ points. If you should hold all five of the top honors, your bonus is _____ points. Where are these bonus points entered on the score sheet? _____

14. How many points are awarded for defeating a contract down 8, doubled, not vulnerable? _____ down 4 on a doubled vulnerable bid? _____

15. How do you compute the score for going down redoubled? _____

30

31

ANSWERS TO QUIZ NO. 2

1.

WE	THEY

2. 20 points

3. 30 points

4. 40 points
   30 points

5. 100 points

6. part score or partial

7. Draw an arrow toward the side that won the game.

8. vulnerable

9. two out of three games

10. 700 points
    500 points

11. overtricks

12. 750 points
    500 points
    1500 points
    1000 points

13. 100 points
    150 points
    above the line

14. 2000 points
    1100 points

15. Multiply the penalty for going down doubled by 2.

Chapter 3
THE OPENING BID

After you have been dealt your 13 cards, the first item on the agenda, after sorting the cards into suits, is to determine whether your hand is of sufficient strength to open the bidding. The number of total points (high-card points plus distributional points) which you must have in order to open the bidding is 13.

Let's assume that you deal and give yourself the following hand:

♠ A Q 10
♡ K 5 4 3
◊ 9 8 7 6
♣ 5 2

You have nine points in high cards plus one distributional point for a total of 10 points. You do not have sufficient strength for an opening bid and you therefore PASS.

Now let's change the above hand slightly:

♠ A Q 10
♡ K 5 4 3
◊ A 8 7 6
♣ 5 2

Counting your points again, you see that you have 13 points in high cards and one distributional point for a total of 14 points. You will, therefore, open the bidding.

WHAT DO I OPEN?

In bridge, the purpose of bidding is to describe the contents of your hand to your partner. Your partner will also bid in an effort to describe his holding. The purpose of this bidding dialogue is to enable you and your partner to decide in what suit and how high to play each hand. You always want to be as descriptive as possible when making a bid and you therefore follow certain rules so that partner will know as nearly as possi-

33

ble what you have when you have made a particular bid.

You will recall from Chapter 1 that spades and hearts are called major suits and that diamonds and clubs are called minor suits. Major suits count more in the scoring than do minor suits and are also higher-ranking. Major suits are therefore given greater emphasis in the bidding than minor suits.

HANDS OF 13-21 POINTS

The first point range for opening bids with which we will deal is the range of 13-21 points. The range between 13 and 21 points will encompass the vast majority of all opening bids which you will ever make. Assuming that you have counted your points and have at least 13 but not more than 21, follow this procedure in order to determine your proper opening bid:

Step 1: Look for your longest suit. If your longest suit is a major suit that contains five or more cards, look no further. Open the bidding one of your major suit. If you hold two five-card majors, open 1 ♠. If you have a five-card major and a five-card minor, bid one of your major. Do not open one of a major unless the major is at least five cards long.

If your longest suit is a four-card major, do not bid one of your major.

EXAMPLE: You hold

♠ 9 8
♡ A Q 10 5 2
♢ A Q 4 3
♣ 5 2

It is your turn to bid. You first count your points. You determine that you have 12 points in high cards and two distributional points for a total of 14 points. You have sufficient points to open the bidding. Applying Step 1, you look for your longest suit. It is a major. Is it at least five cards in length? Yes. You see that you have a five-card heart suit. Your proper opening bid is 1 ♡.

MAJOR

WORTH 30 POINTS

MINOR

WORTH 20 POINTS

35

Step 2: If your longest suit is not a major suit with five or more cards, open the minor suit which contains the most cards.

EXAMPLE: You hold

♠ 5 2
♡ A Q 10 2
♢ A Q 5 3
♣ 9 8 7

You first count your points and determine that you have 12 points in high cards plus one distributional point for a total of 13 points. You have sufficient strength to open the bidding. Applying Step 1, you look first for your longest suit. In this case, you have two four-card suits, one major and one minor. You cannot open 1♠ or 1♡ since you don't have a five-card (or longer) major. You then proceed to Step 2 and look for the minor suit containing the most cards. That suit is, of course, diamonds, and your proper opening bid with the above hand is 1♢.

Step 3: If your longest suit is not a five-card major suit under Step 1, and in applying Step 2 you determine that both of your minor suits are of equal length, you must then apply Step 3. The rule, stated simply, is this:

> If your longest suit is not a five-card major suit and you must open the bidding with a minor suit, open with your longer minor suit. If both of your minor suits are of equal length, open the bidding with 1♢ if you are four-four, five-five, or six-six in the minors, but open 1♣ if you are three-three in the minors.

EXAMPLE: You hold

♠ 5 2
♡ A K 5
◇ 9 8 3 2
♣ A J 5 3

You first add up your points and determine that you have a total of 12 high-card points and one distributional point, a total of 13 points. You have sufficient strength to open the bidding. Applying Step 1, since you have only two spades and three hearts, you obviously cannot open the bidding with 1 ♡ or 1 ♠. You then proceed to Step 2, which is to determine which of your minor suits has the most cards in it. However, you can see that you have four cards in each minor suit. That being the case, you proceed to Step 3. With two four-card minors, you open 1 ◇.

At this point, you should deal several practice hands and use the accompanying chart to assist you in practicing your opening one bids.

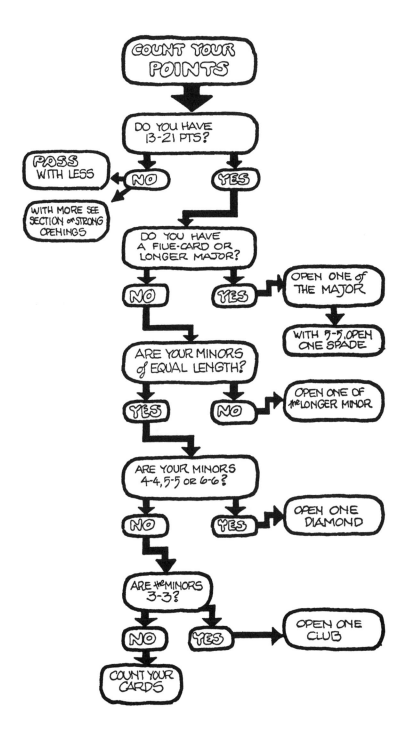

OPENING BIDS OF 1 OF A SUIT

REQUIREMENTS: 13 to 21 points
With less than 13 points...PASS!
With 13-21 points, apply the following steps:

Step 1: Look for your longest suit. If it is a five-card or longer major suit, open the bidding with one of that major suit (with 5 spades and 5 hearts, open 1 ♠).

Step 2: If the longest suit in the hand is not a major suit of five or more cards, open the minor suit with the most cards in it.

Step 3: If the longest suit in the hand is not a major suit of five or more cards and the minor suits are of equal length, open 1 ◊ with four-four, five-five, or six-six in the minor suits, but open 1 ♣ with three-three in the minor suits.

QUIZ NO. 3

For each of the following, answer:
(a) How many points do you have?
(b) What is your opening bid?

1. ♠ A Q J 5 2   (a)_____
   ♡ 9 8 7   (b)_____
   ◊ A 4 3 2
   ♣ 2

2. ♠ 5 3 2   (a)_____
   ♡ K J 10 7 5 2   (b)_____
   ◊ None
   ♣ A K 5 3

3. ♠ K Q J 4 2   (a)_____
   ♡ 5   (b)_____
   ◊ A K Q 9 8
   ♣ 6 4

4. ♠ 9 7   (a)_____
   ♡ J 9 4 3 2   (b)_____
   ◊ 5
   ♣ A K Q J 5

5. ♠ A 5 2   (a)_____
   ♡ K 4 3   (b)_____
   ◊ Q J 3 2
   ♣ A 10 3

6. ♠ K Q 3   (a)_____
   ♡ 9   (b)_____
   ◊ A K 9 8
   ♣ J 5 4 3 2

7. ♠ A K 4 3   (a)_____
   ♡ A K 9 8   (b)_____
   ◊ 5 4 2
   ♣ J 5

8. ♠ Q 9 8 5 4   (a)_____
   ♡ 7   (b)_____
   ◊ A Q 10 8
   ♣ 5 4 3

9. ♠ 8   (a)_____
   ♡ 6 5 4 3 2   (b)_____
   ◊ A K Q J 5
   ♣ 9 8

10. ♠ 6 4   (a)_____
   ♡ A Q 5   (b)_____
   ◊ J 9 8 2
   ♣ A Q 5 4

ANSWERS TO QUIZ NO. 3

1. (a) 13
   (b) 1 ♠

2. (a) 14
   (b) 1 ♥

3. (a) 18
   (b) 1 ♠

4. (a) 14
   (b) 1 ♥

5. (a) 14
   (b) 1 ♦

6. (a) 15
   (b) 1 ♣

7. (a) 15
   (b) 1 ♦

8. (a) 10
   (b) Pass

9. (a) 13
   (b) 1 ♥

10. (a) 14
    (b) 1 ♦

Chapter 4
OTHER OPENING SUIT BIDS

Occasionally you may pick up a hand containing more than 21 points. You cannot open this hand 1♣, 1◊, 1♡, or 1♠ because, as you know, these bids promise 13-21 points. How do you handle these stronger hands?

THE STRONG TWO BID

With 22 or more points, open the bidding with two of your longest suit, provided that you have a five-card or longer suit.

Example 1: You hold   ♠ A 5 2
                               ♡ A K Q 10 5
                               ◊ A K 5 4
                               ♣ A

                               Opening bid: 2♡

Example 2: You hold   ♠ K Q 5
                               ♡ A K 4
                               ◊ A K Q 10 5 2
                               ♣ 2

                               Opening bid: 2◊

Example 3: You hold   ♠ K Q J 10 2
                               ♡ A K 4 3
                               ◊ A K Q 10
                               ♣ None
                               Opening bid: 2♠

PREEMPTIVE BIDDING

You now know how to open the bidding on hands containing 13-21 points and on hands containing 22 or more points. There are occasions, however, on which you will want to open the bidding with less than 13 points. This is done when you hold a very long suit and a weak hand with few points (i.e., less than 10 HCPs). The purpose of opening the bidding on such hands is to

A STRONG TWO

disrupt the opponents' bidding dialogue.

Preemptive opening bids are defined as opening bids made at the three level or higher in spades, hearts, diamonds, or clubs. These bids promise a suit of at least seven cards and a hand containing 3-9 high-card points. The following are examples of preemptive opening bids:

1. ♠ K Q J 10 5 4 3
   ♡ 2
   ◊ J 5 2
   ♣ 9 8
   Opening bid: 3 ♠

2. ♠ 5 2
   ♡ 6 4
   ◊ A Q 10 9 5 4 3
   ♣ 5 2
   Opening bid: 3 ◊

3. ♠ 5 2
   ♡ 4
   ◊ J 2
   ♣ K J 10 6 5 4 3 2
   Opening bid: 3 ♣

Most new players are very hesitant about making preemptive bids. I urge you to adopt the opposite approach—be aggressive and preempt as often as possible. Your long-term gain from such bids will far exceed the occasional losses you will sustain.

QUIZ NO. 4

For each of the following, find your proper opening bid.

1. ♠ None   Opening bid _____
   ♡ A K Q 10 9 8
   ◊ A K Q 2
   ♣ A 5 2

2. ♠ A K Q 9 7 5 2   Opening bid _____
   ♡ 9
   ◇ 8 5
   ♣ Q 5 4

3. ♠ 9   Opening bid _____
   ♡ 7 5
   ◇ K J 10 8 7 5 2
   ♣ Q 5 4

4. ♠ 2   Opening bid _____
   ♡ K Q J 10 5 4 2
   ◇ 9 8
   ♣ 5 4 2

5. ♠ 9   Opening bid _____
   ♡ A
   ◇ A Q J 10 8 7
   ♣ A K Q 10 2

ANSWERS TO QUIZ NO. 4

1. 2♡

2. 1♠

3. 3◊

4. 3♡

5. 2◊

Chapter 5
THE NOTRUMP EXCEPTION

Consider what you have learned to date. You now know that you can open the bidding one of a suit with 13-21 points and that you can open the bidding two of a suit with 22 or more points. Further, with certain hands containing very long suits, you can sometimes make a preemptive bid by opening the bidding at the three level or higher with less than 13 points. A natural question presents itself: Are there any other opening bids?

We now turn our attention to these other opening bids. We consider in this chapter the opening bids of 1 Notrump, 2 Notrump, and 3 Notrump.

GENERAL REQUIREMENTS FOR ANY NOTRUMP OPENING BID

If we elect to play a hand in notrump, we know that there is no trump suit. To open the bidding 1 Notrump, 2 Notrump, or 3 Notrump, you should have a *notrump hand*.

A notrump hand is any hand containing no voids, no singletons, and no suit of six or more cards in length. The final requirement for a notrump hand is that it not contain two doubletons.

Examples of notrump hands are as follows:

1. You hold   ♠ 5 4 2
               ♡ 7 6 5
               ♢ 8 5 4 2
               ♣ 6 4 3

2. You hold   ♠ A K Q 10
               ♡ A K 5 2
               ♢ A K 3
               ♣ A Q

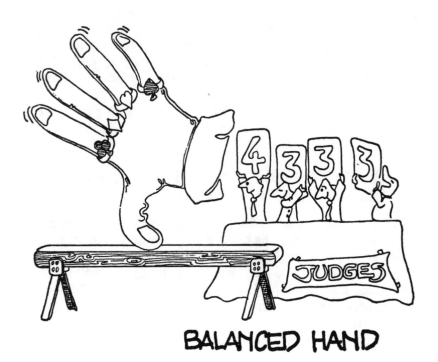

BALANCED HAND

3. You hold   ♠ 5 4 3 2
            ♥ A J
            ♦ K Q 4 3
            ♣ 8 5 2

4. You hold   ♠ 5 4 2
            ♥ 6 3 2
            ♦ J 9 7 5 4
            ♣ 5 2

Examine the above hands. You will note that it does not matter how many points are in the hand in determining whether or not the hand is a notrump hand. Rather, the only important factor in making this determination is the *pattern* (or distribution) of the cards.

Each of the four hands below is not a notrump hand. Decide why before reading further.

1. You hold   ♠ A K 8 7 5 2
            ♥ Q 9 7
            ♦ 5 4
            ♣ 9 7

2. You hold   ♠ J 7 5 4 2
            ♥ K Q 9 8
            ♦ None
            ♣ 9 8 6 2

3. You hold   ♠ 9
            ♥ K Q 5 4
            ♦ A Q 10 9
            ♣ K J 4 2

4. You hold   ♠ 9 8
            ♥ 8 5
            ♦ A K 5 4 2
            ♣ A K Q 2

Hand 1 is not a notrump hand because it contains a six-card suit and because it contains two doubletons. Hand 2 is not a

notrump hand because it contains a void. Hand 3 fails because it contains a singleton. Hand 4 fails to qualify because it contains two doubletons.

IMPORTANT: In evaluating a hand for a notrump contract, count only high-card points. Do not count distributional points.

OPENING BID OF 1 NOTRUMP

The opening bid of 1 Notrump requires a holding of 16-18 points **in high cards only** and a notrump-type hand. Examples of 1 Notrump opening bids are as follows:

1. You hold   ♠ A 5 4 2
           ♡ A Q 9
           ◊ K 3 2
           ♣ A 5 4

2. You hold   ♠ K 5 4
           ♡ K Q 10 9
           ◊ K 5 4 3
           ♣ A J

3. You hold   ♠ K 2
           ♡ Q 5 4
           ◊ A Q 10 9 2
           ♣ A K 4

Note that each of the foregoing hands is a hand of the notrump type and contains 16-18 high-card points.

OPENING BID OF 2 NOTRUMP

The requirements for a 2 Notrump opener are a notrump-type hand with 22-24 high-card points. Examples of hands which should be opened 2 Notrump are as follows:

1. You hold   ♠ A Q 10
           ♡ K J 9 2
           ◊ A K 4
           ♣ A Q 3

2. You hold ♠ A K 4 2
      ♡ A Q 5 2
      ◊ K J
      ♣ A J 2

3. You hold ♠ K Q 5
      ♡ K J 2
      ◊ A K J 9 8
      ♣ A Q

The proper opening bid on all of the above hands is 2 Notrump.

OPENING BID OF 3 NOTRUMP

To open the bidding 3 Notrump requires a notrump-type pattern with 25-27 high-card points. Should you be fortunate enough to hold a hand such as the three below, your proper opening bid would be 3 Notrump.

1. You hold ♠ A K 2
      ♡ K Q 10 4
      ◊ A K 5
      ♣ A Q 9

2. You hold ♠ A Q J 2
      ♡ K Q J 9
      ◊ A K 2
      ♣ A Q

3. You hold ♠ A Q 5
      ♡ A J 2
      ◊ A Q
      ♣ A K J 5 4

The astute observer will realize that we have now discussed all opening bids from 1 ♣ through 3 Notrump. In finding your proper opening bid, the opening bids of 1 Notrump, 2 Notrump, and 3 Notrump should be bid in preference to opening suit bids. The accompanying chart indicates the procedures I recommend you follow to most readily find your appropriate opening bid on any hand.

PROCEDURE TO DETERMINE WHAT TO OPEN

Step 1: Arrange your cards into suits.

Step 2: Determine whether your hand is of the notrump type.

Step 3: Count your high-card points and your distributional points. If you have enough points to open the bidding *and* a notrump-type hand, then check to see whether your number of high-card points fits the requirements for opening bids of 1, 2 or 3 Notrump. If so, open the bidding the appropriate number of notrump. If not, follow the steps outlined for opening bids of 1 of a suit set out in the chart on page 40.

Note that if your hand is of the notrump type, it is preferable to open a notrump bid even if you have a five-card major.

This concludes our discussion of all the opening bids in the game of bridge. Quiz No. 5 tests your knowledge of all opening bids.

QUIZ NO. 5

For each of the following hands indicate your proper opening bid:

1. You hold ♠ A Q 2
   ♡ J 10 4 3
   ◊ K Q 5
   ♣ A 4 2
   Opening bid _____

2. You hold ♠ A Q 10 5 4
            ♡ 5
            ◊ A J 9 8
            ♣ K 10 4

Opening bid _____

3. You hold ♠ K 3 2
            ♡ Q
            ◊ A K J 5 4
            ♣ J 4 3 2

Opening bid _____

4. You hold ♠ K J 2
            ♡ A K 4 2
            ◊ A Q J
            ♣ A J 2

Opening bid _____

5. You hold ♠ 2
            ♡ A K Q J 7
            ◊ A K 9 8
            ♣ K Q 2

Opening bid _____

6. You hold ♠ K Q 4 3
            ♡ 5 3 2
            ◊ 2
            ♣ A K Q 5 4

Opening bid _____

7. You hold ♠ A Q J 2
            ♡ K Q 3
            ◊ K Q J
            ♣ A K 2

Opening bid _____

8. You hold ♠ 3 2
   ♡ K Q J 10 5 4 3
   ◊ 2
   ♣ 5 4 2
Opening bid _____

9. You hold ♠ 7 6 3
   ♡ A K J 5 4
   ◊ A Q 4 2
   ♣ 2
Opening bid _____

10. You hold ♠ K J 4
    ♡ A J 2
    ◊ K 5 4 3 2
    ♣ A J
Opening bid _____

11. You hold ♠ 10 5 4 3 2
    ♡ K Q J 5
    ◊ K Q 5 2
    ♣ None
Opening bid _____

12. You hold ♠ A Q 4 2
    ♡ A Q J 2
    ◊ K J
    ♣ A Q 4
Opening bid _____

13. You hold ♠ 2
    ♡ 5 4
    ◊ A K J 10 5 3 2
    ♣ 5 4 2
Opening bid _____

14. You hold ♠ A Q 2
          ♡ K 5 4
          ◊ K 5 4 2
          ♣ Q 3 2
Opening bid _____

15. You hold ♠ A K
          ♡ K Q 4
          ◊ K Q J 10 2
          ♣ A K J
Opening bid _____

16. You hold ♠ A Q J 2
          ♡ 3 2
          ◊ Q J 2
          ♣ A 4 3 2
Opening bid _____

17. You hold ♠ A
          ♡ A K Q 5 4 2
          ◊ K Q J 2
          ♣ A 2
Opening bid _____

18. You hold ♠ 2
          ♡ A Q 5 4 2
          ◊ A Q 5 4 2
          ♣ 3 2
Opening bid _____

ANSWERS TO QUIZ NO. 5

1. 1 Notrump

2. 1 ♠

3. 1 ◇

4. 2 Notrump

5. 2 ♡

6. 1 ♣

7. 3 Notrump

8. 3 ♡

9. 1 ♡

10. 1 Notrump

11. 1 ♠

12. 2 Notrump

13. 3 ◇

14. 1 ◇

15. 3 Notrump

16. 1 ♣

17. 2 ♡

18. 1 ♡

Chapter 6
GAMES AND SLAMS

Bidding in bridge is nothing more or less than an attempt to tell your partner in code form what the laws of bridge forbid you to tell him in common language. For example, assume you hold the following hand:

♠ A Q 5 4 2
♡ 5
◊ K 4 3 2
♣ A 5 4

It would be simple to look at your partner and say, "Partner, I have a five-card spade suit and sufficient points to open the bidding." However, the laws of bridge do not permit you to address your partner in this fashion. You must, therefore, relay the contents of your hand to partner through bidding. The message above can be conveyed to partner by saying "1♠".

PURPOSE OF THE BIDDING DIALOGUE

The purpose of bidding is to exchange information with partner so that the two of you may determine in what suit and how high to play each contract. You may be able to determine very easily that neither of you should be bidding. For example, if each of you holds four points, neither of you will usually do anything throughout the entire auction other than pass. On the other hand, if each of you has very strong holdings, the auction may require several bids by you and your partner to fully describe the contents of both hands.

Basically, the more you bid in bridge, the more you score if you make it. If you and your partner bid high enough and make your contract, you may also score premium points for bidding *game* or *slam*.

WHAT IS A GAME BID?

The partnership may bid game in any of the suits or in

notrump. A contract of 3 Notrump (nine tricks) is a game bid in notrump, 4♡ (10 tricks) and 4♠ (10 tricks) are game bids in the major suits, and 5♣ (11 tricks) and 5♢ (11 tricks) are game bids in the minor suits. It is desirable for the partnership to bid and make games whenever possible. If you and your partner succeed in bidding and making a game contract, you will score extra points for your success.

Sometimes you and your partner may hold sufficient strength to enable you to contract for 12 or 13 tricks. Bidding and making a six level contract (12 tricks) is called making a *small slam*. Bidding and making all 13 tricks is called a *grand slam*. Premium points in addition to premiums for game bids are awarded if you are able to successfully bid and make a small or grand slam.

HOW DO WE KNOW WHETHER TO BID GAME OR SLAM?

In order to have a reasonable expectation of making a game contract, the *combined* assets in your hand *and* in partner's hand should total at least 26 points. You will have a reasonable expectation of making 3 Notrump, 4♡, or 4♠ if you and your partner have 26 or more points.

To make game in either of the minor suits (5♣ or 5♢), you and your partner should have combined strength of at least 29 points.

To make a small slam (12 tricks), you and your partner should have combined strength of at least 33 points.

Finally, to have a reasonable expectation of making a grand slam (all 13 tricks) you and your partner should have combined strength of at least 37 points.

The chart on page 63 summarizes the requirements for game and slam bids. You should learn these important numbers.

POINT REQUIREMENTS TO BID GAMES AND SLAMS

Game Contract	Points Required To Have A Reasonable Expectation To Make
1. 3 Notrump	26 points (high-card points only)
2. 4♡	26 points
3. 4♠	26 points
4. 5♣	29 points
5. 5◇	29 points

Slams	Points Required To Have A Reasonable Expectation To Make
1. Small slam (12 tricks) ....33 points
2. Grand slam (13 tricks)....37 points

QUIZ NO. 6

1. To bid a game contract in hearts or spades, you must bid _____ or _____.

2. To bid a game contract in clubs or diamonds, you must bid _____ or _____.

3. To bid a game contract in notrump, you must bid _____.

4. To make a game contract in notrump, the partnership must win at least _____ tricks.

5. To make a game contract in hearts, the partnership must win at least _____ tricks.

THE LATEST IN GAMES

A FASCINATING GAME PLAYED TOTALLY WITHOUT TRUMP. OBJECT~ TO WIN NINE TRICKS.

VALUE : 100 POINTS
OUR PRICE : 26 HCP

AN ACTION-PACKED CHASE GAME WHERE YOU RACE TO WIN 10 TRICKS BEFORE THE ENEMY WINS FOUR.

VALUE : 120 POINTS
OUR PRICE : 26 HCP

A MINOR-SUITED GAME OF SKILL WHERE YOU, AS DECLARER, MUST WIN ELEVEN TRICKS.

VALUE: 100 POINTS
OUR PRICE : 29 HCP

more games from the world of BRIDGE

6. To make a game contract in spades, the partnership must win at least _____ tricks.

7. To make a game contract in diamonds, the partnership must win at least _____ tricks.

8. To make a game contract in clubs, the partnership must win at least _____ tricks.

9. To bid and make a small slam, the partnership should have a combined strength of at least _____ points.

10. To bid and make a grand slam, the partnership should have a combined strength of at least _____ points.

11. To bid and make a small slam, the partnership must contract for and make _____ tricks.

12. To bid and make a grand slam, the partnership must contract for and make _____ tricks.

13. To bid and make a game in either major suit, the partnership should have a combined strength of at least _____ points.

14. To bid and make a game in either minor suit, the partnership should have a combined strength of at least _____ points.

15. To bid and make a game in notrump, the partnership should have a combined strength of at least _____ points in high cards only.

ANSWERS TO QUIZ NO. 6

1. 4♡ or 4♠

2. 5♣ or 5◊

3. 3 Notrump

4. 9

5. 10

6. 10

7. 11

8. 11

9. 33 points

10. 37 points

11. 12 tricks

12. 13 tricks

13. 26 points

14. 29 points

15. 26 points

Chapter 7
RESPONSES TO OPENING SUIT BIDS

In this chapter, we deal with *responses* to opening bids. To set the stage, assume that you have picked up your cards, sorted them into suits, and evaluated your hand by counting your points. Your partner is the first to speak and opens the bidding with one of the opening bids outlined in previous chapters. By opening the bidding, your partner has given you a message regarding the nature and strength of his hand. Assume that the opponent sitting on your right passes. It is now your turn to bid and your bid is called a *response.*

WHAT DO I NEED TO RESPOND?

To answer this question, we must first know what partner's opening bid was. Just as we categorized all of the possible opening bids in previous chapters, we shall likewise categorize the appropriate responses according to what opening bid partner made.

RESPONSES TO OPENING BIDS OF
1♡ OR 1♠

When partner opens the bidding with one in a major suit (1♡ or 1♠), the following rules apply:

A. With 0-5 points, pass.

B. With 6-9 points, apply the following steps:

1. First, check to see if you have 3 or more cards in partner's major suit. If so, raise partner's major suit to the two level.
    Example: You hold   ♠ K 5 2
                          ♡ J 8 7 6
                          ◊ 3 2
                          ♣ A 7 6 2
    Partner's opening bid: 1 ♠
    Your response: 2 ♠

2. With 6-9 points and two or less cards in your partner's suit, bid a four-card or longer major suit at the one level if you are able to do so.
    Example: You hold   ♠ K 9 3 2
                          ♡ 5 2
                          ◊ K 5 4 2
                          ♣ 9 8 7
    Partner's opening bid: 1 ♡
    Your response: 1 ♠

3. With 6-9 high-card points, two or less cards in partner's suit, and no major suit of four or more cards that can be bid at the one level, bid 1 Notrump.
    Example: You hold   ♠ 9 2
                          ♡ J
                          ◊ Q 10 5 4 2
                          ♣ A 6 4 3 2
    Partner's opening bid: 1 ♡
    Your response: 1 Notrump

C. With 10-12 points, apply the following steps:

1. Bid a major suit of four or more cards if you can do so at the one level.
    Example: You hold   ♠ K Q 5 4
                          ♡ J 5
                          ◊ A 4 3 2
                          ♣ 9 5 3
    Partner's opening bid: 1 ♡
    Your response: 1 ♠

2. Bid a new suit at the two level.
   Example: You hold ♠ 9 3
                        ♡ K 5 2
                        ◊ A K 4 3 2
                        ♣ 5 4 3
   Partner's opening bid: 1 ♡
   Your response: 2 ◊

D. With 13-15 points, apply the following steps:

1. With four or more cards in partner's suit, raise his suit to the three level.
   Example: You hold ♠ K 4 3 2
                        ♡ A 4 3 2
                        ◊ 8 6
                        ♣ A Q 5
   Partner's opening bid: 1 ♠
   Your response: 3 ♠

2. With 13-15 points and three or less cards in your partner's suit, bid your longest suit. If you have two suits of equal length, bid the major first. If you have two minors of equal length, bid 2 ◊.
   Example: You hold ♠ A K 9 3 2
                        ♡ 6 3
                        ◊ K 6 5
                        ♣ K 8 3
   Partner's opening bid: 1 ♡
   Your response: 1 ♠

   Example: You hold ♠ 8 4
                        ♡ K 9
                        ◊ A K Q 3 2
                        ♣ 6 5 3 2
   Partner's opening bid: 1 ♡
   Your response: 2 ◊

3. Bid 2 Notrump with a notrump-type hand and 13-15 HCPs.

Example: You hold ♠ Q 5 2
♡ J 2
◊ A Q 5 2
♣ K J 4 3

Partner's opening bid: 1 ♡
Your response: 2 Notrump

E. With 16-18 points, apply the following steps:

1. With 16-18 points, bid your longest suit at the lowest possible level. If you have two suits of equal length, bid a major if one of the suits is a major; if both suits are minors, bid 2 ◊.

Example: You hold ♠ A K Q 3 2
♡ 7 2
◊ K Q 4
♣ Q 9 5

Partner's opening bid: 1 ♡
Your response: 1 ♠

Example: You hold ♠ K 4
♡ A 10 8
◊ A K Q 5 3
♣ 8 6 4

Partner's opening bid: 1 ♡
Your response: 2 ◊

2. *Jump shift* with 19 or more points and a good suit of your own or good (i.e., four-card or longer) support for partner's suit.

NOTE: A jump shift is a bid in a new suit that skips one level of bidding.

Examples of jump shifts are as follows:

Partner opens	Jump shift response
1. 1 ♡	3 ♣
2. 1 ♠	3 ◊
3. 1 ♡	2 ♠

Example: You hold   ♠ 5 2
                     ♡ A Q 3
                     ◊ A K Q 9 4 2
                     ♣ K 8

Partner's opening bid: 1 ♠
Your response: 3 ◊

3. With 16-18 points, a notrump-type hand, and no four-card or longer major, bid 3 Notrump.

Example: You hold   ♠ K Q 2
                     ♡ J 2
                     ◊ A Q 4 3
                     ♣ K J 5 2

Partner's opening bid: 1 ♡
Your response: 3 Notrump

RESPONSES TO OPENING BIDS OF 1 OF A MINOR (1♣ or 1◊)

A. With 0-5 points, pass.

B. With 6-9 points, apply the following steps:

1. First, look for your longest suit. If you can bid that suit at the one level, bid one of your suit. If you have two suits of equal length—two four-card suits—bid the lower-ranking suit (providing you can bid it at the one level); if you have two five- or six-card suits, bid the higher-ranking suit (providing you can do so at the one level).

a) Example: You hold ♠ K 5 4 2
                     ♡ J 3 2
                     ◊ K 5
                     ♣ 9 4 3 2

Partner's opening bid: 1 ◊
Your response: 1 ♠

"I'M BEGINNING TO GET THE
HANG OF IT. BRIDGE IS AN
EASY GAME—SOMETIMES."

b) Example: You hold ♠ K 6 4 3
                  ♡ J 8 7 2
                  ◊ K 3
                  ♣ 9 5 2
Partner's opening bid: 1 ◊
Your response: 1 ♡

c) Example: You hold ♠ K 6 4 3 2
                  ♡ J 8 7 4 2
                  ◊ Q 7
                  ♣ 6
Partner's opening bid: 1 ◊
Your response: 1 ♠

2. If you have no four-card major suit and cannot respond under Step 1 above, next check to see if you have four or more cards in partner's minor suit. If so, raise partner's minor suit to the two level.

Example: You hold   ♠ K 2
                    ♡ 5 4
                    ◊ A 4 3 2
                    ♣ 9 8 6 4 3
Partner's opening bid: 1 ◊
Your response: 2 ◊

3. If you have no four-card or longer suit that you can bid at the one level and also lack four or more cards in partner's suit, respond 1 Notrump with 6-9 high-card points.

Example: You hold   ♠ Q 4 3
                    ♡ J 2
                    ◊ Q 6 5
                    ♣ K 10 4 3 2
Partner's opening bid: 1 ◊
Your response: 1 Notrump

73

C. With 10-12 points, apply the following steps:

    1. Bid your longest suit if you can do so at the one level. If you cannot bid your longest suit at the one level, then bid another suit of four or more cards at the one level.

Example: You hold   ♠ J 4 2
                    ♡ K Q 10 7
                    ◊ A 4 2
                    ♣ 8 4 3

Partner's opening bid: 1 ♣
Your response: 1 ♡

    2. If you cannot bid a suit at the one level, bid your longest suit at the two level.

Example: You hold   ♠ K 2
                    ♡ 5 4 3
                    ◊ 6 4 2
                    ♣ A K 9 7 5

Partner's opening bid: 1 ◊
Your response: 2 ♣

D. With 13-15 points, apply the following steps:

    1. Bid your longest suit at the lowest possible level.

Example: You hold   ♠ Q 6 5
                    ♡ A K 10 5
                    ◊ A 9 7
                    ♣ 6 5 2

Partner's opening bid: 1 ◊
Your response: 1 ♡ \

Example: You hold   ♠ 5 2
                    ♡ A 5
                    ◊ 5 4 2
                    ♣ A K J 6 4 3

Partner's opening bid: 1 ◊
Your response: 2 ♣

2. Bid 2 Notrump with a notrump-type hand.
   Example: You hold   ♠ K 5 3
                            ♡ J 3 2
                            ◊ K 4 3 2
                            ♣ A Q 5
   Partner's opening bid: 1 ♣
   Your response: 2 Notrump

E. With 16-18 points, bid your longest suit at the lowest possible level, or bid 3 Notrump with a notrump-type hand.

F. With 19 or more points, you should jump shift.

RESPONSES TO OPENING BIDS OF 2♣, 2◊, 2♡, AND 2♠

On those rare occasions when you are fortunate enough to have partner open the bidding with two of a suit, and irrespective of which strong two bid your partner might open, your responses are as follows:

A. With 0-5 points, bid 2 Notrump (negative response).

B. With 6-8 points, raise partner's suit to the three level with three or more cards in his suit. If you do not have at least three cards in partner's suit, bid any suit of your own containing five or more cards. With less than three cards in partner's suit and no suit of five or more cards of your own, bid 3 Notrump.

C. With 9 or more points, you should consider bidding a small slam or grand slam. Slam bidding is discussed in detail in Chapter 14.

RESPONSES TO OPENING BIDS OF 3♣, 3◊, 3♡, AND 3♠

You will recall that partner may, on occasion, open the bidding with a *preemptive bid* and that such bids commonly show a weak hand with a very long suit. How do you respond to such an opening?

When partner has opened with a preemptive bid, your normal response will be to pass. We know that 26 points are generally required between your hand and partner's hand in order to bid and make game. When partner has opened with a preempt, the maximum number of high-card points he can have is nine and you should normally pass any hand with 16 or less points.

On those occasions when partner preempts and you have 17 or more points in your hand, you should raise your partner's major to game. If your partner has bid a minor, bid 3 Notrump holding a three-card fit in partner's suit and high cards in the other three suits.

You have now learned the appropriate initial response to all opening suit bids. The material which has been covered in this chapter is probably the most difficult material which you will encounter in this book. You should review this material and study with care the examples which have been furnished for your use. Also, at this point, you should definitely be playing as you learn. There is no substitute for at-the-table experience.

Now test your knowledge of responses by answering the questions in Quiz No. 7.

QUIZ NO. 7

In each example below, you hold:

1. ♠ K 8 3 2
   ♡ 5 4
   ◊ J 9 8 3
   ♣ Q 5 4

   A. Partner's opening bid: 1 ♡
      Your response: _____
   B. Partner's opening bid: 1 ♠
      Your response: _____

2. ♠ Q 2
   ♡ J 3 2
   ◊ Q 5 4 3
   ♣ K 7 6 2

   A. Partner's opening bid: 1 ♡
      Your response: _____
   B. Partner's opening bid: 1 ♠
      Your response: _____

3. ♠ Q J 10 5
   ♡ 9 2
   ◊ K 10 7
   ♣ 5 4 3 2

   A. Partner's opening bid: 1 ♡
      Your response: _____
   B. Partner's opening bid: 1 ♠
      Your response: _____

4. ♠ 8 2   A. Partner's opening bid: 1♡ _2 ♣_
   ♡ Q 5 4   Your response: _____
_10_ ◊ A 4 3   B. Partner's opening bid: 1♠
   ♣ K J 10 5 2   Your response: ____ _2 ♣_

5. ♠ J 5 3   A. Partner's opening bid: 1♡ _Pass_ _0-5_
_4_ ♡ J 5 3   Your response: ____ _PASS_
   ◊ Q 10 2   B. Partner's opening bid: 1♠ _PASS_
   ♣ 9 8 6 3   Your response: ____

6. ♠ K 3 2   A. Partner's opening bid: 1♣ _1 H_
_6_ ♡ Q 4 3 2_   Your response: _____
   ◊ J 5 4   B. Partner's opening bid: 1◊ _1 H_
   ♣ 10 9 3   Your response: _____

7. ♠ Q 3   _lowest ranking_   A. Partner's opening bid: 1♣ _1 ♥_
_7_ ♡ J 4 3 2 _ranking_   Your response: _____
   ◊ K J 8 6 _1 minor_   B. Partner's opening bid: 1◊ _1 H_
   ♣ 9 3 2   Your response: _____

8. ♠ J 5 2   A. Partner's opening bid: 1♣ _2 C_
_7_ ♡ Q 4 3   Your response: _____
   ◊ 9 8 2   B. Partner's opening bid: 1◊ _1 NT_
   ♣ K J 5 4   Your response: _____

9. ♠ K Q 10 4   A. Partner's opening bid: 1♣ _1 S_
_8_ ♡ J 8 7   Your response: _____
   ◊ Q 10 8   B. Partner's opening bid: 1◊ _1 S_
   ♣ 10 5 4   Your response: _____

_13-15_ _w/ 4 raise_
10. ♠ K Q 3 2 _To 3_   A. Partner's opening bid: 1♡ _3 H_
_14_ ♡ Q 8 4 2   Your response: _____
   ◊ A 9   B. Partner's opening bid: 1♠ _3 ♠_
   ♣ K 3 2   Your response: _____

11. ♠ Q 2   A. Partner's opening bid: 1♡ _3 H_
_14_ ♡ K 4 3 2   Your response: _____
   ◊ A Q 3 2   B. Partner's opening bid: 1♠ _2 NT_
   ♣ K 9 7   Your response: _____

12. ♠ Q 5 4
   ♡ J 3 2
17 ♢ A K 9 4
   ♣ A Q J

A. Partner's opening bid: 1♣ *3 NT*
   Your response: _____
B. Partner's opening bid: 1♢ *3 NT*
   Your response: _____

13. ♠ K 3
   ♡ 9 8 2
   ♢ A K Q 10 6 4
   ♣ A Q

A. Partner's opening bid: 1♣ *2 ♢*
   Your response: _____
B. Partner's opening bid: 1♠ *3 ♢*
   Your response: _____

18 Bid longest suit at lowest level

14. ♠ 9 7
   ♡ K 4 2
   ♢ A K 9 7 4
11 ♣ J 3 2

A. Partner's opening bid: 1♣
   Your response: _____
B. Partner's opening bid: 1♠
   Your response: _____

suit possible

31

No Trump, even dist., No sing, 1 double, No void

ANSWERS TO QUIZ NO. 7

1. A. 1♠
   B. 2♠

2. A. 2♡
   B. 1 Notrump

3. A. 1♠
   B. 2♠

4. A. 2♣
   B. 2♣

5. A. Pass
   B. Pass

6. A. 1♡
   B. 1♡

7. A. 1♢
   B. 1♡

8. A. 2♣
   B. 1 Notrump

9. A. 1♠
   B. 1♠

10. A. 3♡
    B. 3♠

11. A. 3♡
    B. 2 Notrump

12. A. 3 Notrump
    B. 3 Notrump

13. A. 2♢
    B. 3♢

14. A. 1♢
    B. 2♢

Chapter 8
RESPONSES TO OPENING NOTRUMP BIDS

In the previous chapter, we learned how to respond to partner's opening *suit* bid. In this chapter, we learn how to respond when partner opens *1, 2, or 3 Notrump*.

A quick review of Chapter 5 will refresh your knowledge as to what partner has when he opens the bidding 1, 2, or 3 Notrump. We now take up responses to each of those opening bids.

RESPONSES TO AN OPENING BID OF 1 NOTRUMP

There is great advantage in opening the bidding in notrump for the reason that the opening notrump bidder defines his distribution and the total number of points in his hand within a very narrow range. Since responder knows the opening bidder's strength within a range of three points, the task of responding is greatly simplified.

Assume that partner has opened the bidding 1 Notrump (16-18 high-card points and balanced distribution). Before deciding how to respond, you should first evaluate your hand in order to determine whether a game should be bid. You know that 26 points are required as a minimum for bidding and making a game. Therefore, you know that game should be bid any time you hold 10 or more high-card points opposite your partner's 1 Notrump opening bid. Similarly, whenever you hold a hand containing 0-7 points, you know that game should not be bid since the total of your points and partner's points cannot be more than 25.

The only hands on which you will be uncertain as to whether game should be bid after partner has opened 1 Notrump are those hands in which you hold eight or nine points. If partner has only 16 points for his 1 Notrump opening bid, you do not want to bid game. However, if partner has 18 points for his 1 Notrump bid, you would want to be in game since you have 26 or 27 points in the combined hands.

On those hands in which you have 10 or more high-card

81

points, you know that you will keep the bidding open until a game has been bid. On those hands containing 0-7 high-card points, you will stop the bidding below game. However, since you do not know whether game should be bid on those hands containing eight or nine high-card points, you will bid in such a fashion so as to pass the final decision as to whether to bid game back to partner.

RESPONDING TO 1 NOTRUMP WITH HANDS CONTAINING 0-7 POINTS

In responding to partner's 1 Notrump opening bid with 0-7 high-card points, apply the following rules:

A. If you have five or more cards in diamonds, hearts, or spades, bid two of that suit.

Example 1: You hold ♠ Q 10 5 4 3 2
♡ 2
◊ 5 4 2
♣ 9 8 7

Partner's opening bid: 1 Notrump
Your response: 2 ♠

Example 2: You hold ♠ 5 2
♡ 9 7
◊ Q J 4 3 2
♣ J 4 3 2

Partner's opening bid: 1 Notrump
Your response: 2 ◊

The bids described above are called *sign-off bids*. They tell partner that game should not be bid. Partner must pass these responses. Thus, in the examples shown above, the final contract will be 2 ♠ and 2 ◊, respectively.

B. With any other hand containing 0-7 high-card points, simply pass.

Example 3: You hold ♠ Q 4 3 2
                   ♡ 5 2
                   ◊ J 4 3 2
                   ♣ A 5 4

Partner's opening bid: 1 Notrump
Your response: Pass

Example 4: You hold ♠ J 4 2
                   ♡ K 5
                   ◊ J 5 3 2
                   ♣ 9 8 3 2

Partner's opening bid: 1 Notrump
Your response: Pass

Before moving on to the proper responses to a 1 Notrump opening bid on hands containing eight or more high-card points, let's pause for a moment to look again at Example 1 on the previous page:

You hold   ♠ Q 10 5 4 3 2
                  ♡ 2
                  ◊ 5 4 2
                  ♣ 9 8 7

You may wonder why you should respond at all to partner's 1 Notrump opening bid knowing that you do not have sufficient points for game. Why not pass?

The answer to this query becomes apparent upon examining the heart suit. Note that your hand contains only one small heart. If the opponents should hold the Ace, King, Queen and several other hearts, they would be able to lead the Ace to which partner, as declarer at 1NT, would play your small heart. The opponents could then lead the King and, since partner would be declaring a 1 Notrump contract, nothing would be trump. The opponents could continue to lead hearts until they ran out of hearts and you would not be able to trump those tricks. However, look at what happens if you make the proper response of 2♠ on the above hand. You will be the declarer in a 2♠ contract and, while the opponents may hold Ace, King, and

Queen of hearts, they will only be able to win one trick in hearts. When they lead the Ace of hearts, you will play your small heart, but when they lead the King of hearts, you will play a spade, trumping that trick, and securing that trick for your side.

THE STAYMAN CONVENTION

Many years ago, it was learned that suit contracts in which the combined hands contained eight or more cards in one suit produced on the average 1½ more tricks per hand than a corresponding notrump contract. Since 3 Notrump is a game bid in notrump, while 4 ♡ and 4 ♠ are game bids in hearts and spades, it logically follows that a partnership should prefer to play a heart or spade contract in preference to a notrump contract whenever the combined hands contain a major suit of eight or more cards.

The Stayman Convention was devised to enable the responder to an opening notrump bid to be able to discover whether opener has a four-card major suit. Responder asks opener whether he has a four-card major suit by responding 2♣ to partner's 1 Notrump opening bid. This 2♣ response says nothing about clubs. Instead, it asks partner one question, and one question only: "Partner, do you have a four-card major suit?"

WHEN DO I BID STAYMAN?

Responder should use the Stayman Convention any time he has eight or more points opposite his partner's 1 Notrump opening bid *and* has at least one major suit of four or more cards. For example, if responder holds:

> ♠ K Q 10 2
> ♡ K J
> ◊ Q 4 3 2
> ♣ 5 3 2

and partner opens 1 Notrump, responder should bid 2♣, the Stayman Convention, asking partner whether he has a four-card major suit. If opener indicates that he has a four-card spade suit by bidding 2♠, responder will bid game in spades (4♠). If opener does not have a four-card spade suit, responder will simply bid 3 Notrump.

HOW DOES OPENER ANSWER A STAYMAN INQUIRY?

Assume the bidding has gone as follows:

Opener	Responder
1 Notrump	2♣
?	

Opener has only three possible answers to a Stayman inquiry:

1. 2♦ (no four-card major suit)
2. 2♥ (four-card heart suit, denies holding 4♠)
3. 2♠ (four-card spade suit, may also have 4♥)

If opener holds four cards in both major suits, he should respond to the Stayman inquiry with a bid of 2♠. Then, if partner cannot support spades, opener can later bid hearts.

CONTINUING THE STAYMAN DIALOGUE

When you respond with a Stayman 2♣ bid to partner's 1 Notrump opener, you will have one of three hand types:

1. Invitational hand...................8 to 9 points
2. Game hand......................10 to 14 points
3. Slam hand.....................15 or more points

No matter which of the above hand-types you have, you will, of course, have at least one four-card major suit.

To continue the Stayman dialogue after partner's response to your 2♣ Stayman inquiry, invite partner to game with an invitational hand, bid game with a game hand, and try for slam with a slam hand. If partner's response to your Stayman inquiry hits your four-card major suit, raise that major suit to the three level with an invitational hand, bid four of that major suit with a game hand, and bid a slam with a slam hand. Conversely, if partner's response to your Stayman inquiry does not uncover a 4-4 major suit fit, invite game with an invitational hand by bidding 2 Notrump, bid 3 Notrump with a game hand, and bid a slam with a slam hand. Below are some examples illustrative of typical Stayman sequences:

Example 1: Responder holds
♠ K J 4 2
♡ K 3 2
◊ K J 3 2
♣ 9 7

Opener	Responder
1 NT	2♣
2♠	4♠

Example 2: Responder holds
♠ K J 4 2
♡ K 3 2
◊ K J 3 2
♣ 9 7

Opener	Responder
1 NT	2♣
2♡	3 NT

Example 3: Responder holds
♠ K J 4 2
♡ 9 3 2
◊ K J 3 2
♣ 9 7

Opener	Responder
1 NT	2♣
2◊	2 NT

Example 4: Responder holds:
♠ K J 4 2
♡ 9 3 2
◊ K J 3 2
♣ 9 7

Opener	Responder
1 NT	2♣
2♠	3♠

Example 5: Responder holds   ♠ K Q 10 2
                                    ♡ K 6
                                    ◊ A J 8 2
                                    ♣ A 10 2

Opener	Responder
1 NT	2♣
2♠	6♠

Example 6: Responder holds   ♠ K Q 10 2
                                    ♡ K 6
                                    ◊ A J 8 2
                                    ♣ A 10 2

Opener	Responder
1 NT	2♣
2♡	6 NT

Example 7: Responder holds   ♠ K Q 10 2
                                    ♡ K 6
                                    ◊ A J 8 2
                                    ♣ A 10 2

Opener	Responder
1 NT	2♣
2◊	6 NT

OTHER RESPONSES TO 1 NOTRUMP

If partner opens 1 Notrump and you hold a balanced hand containing eight or nine high-card points without a four-card major, you should not use the Stayman Convention. Instead, simply raise partner directly to 2 Notrump and let partner decide whether to carry on to game. Should you hold 10-14 high-card points, raise partner directly to 3 Notrump. With 15 or 16 high-card points, a balanced hand, and no four-card major suit, raise partner's 1 Notrump opening bid to 4 Notrump, which asks partner to bid a small slam in notrump if he has a maximum 1 Notrump opening bid. With 17 or 18 high-card points, raise partner directly to 6 Notrump. With 21 or more high-card points, raise partner directly to 7 Notrump. With 19 or 20 high-card points, raise partner to 5 Notrump, which invites partner to bid 7 Notrump if he has a maximum 1 Notrump opening bid.

WHAT ABOUT UNBALANCED HANDS?

With an unbalanced hand and 10 or more points, you know that you still want to bid game but you have to figure out whether to play in a suit or in notrump. When you have 10 or more points and a major suit of five cards, you should respond with three of your major suit. Lacking three-card or longer support for your suit, partner will bid 3 Notrump. With three-card or longer support, partner will raise your suit to game.

Example 1: Responder holds
♠ A K J 4 2
♥ Q 5
♦ Q 10 4 2
♣ 5 3

Opener	Responder
1 NT	3 ♠

Example 2: Responder holds
♠ 9 4 2
♥ K Q J 9 7
♦ A 3
♣ 9 8 7

Opener	Responder
1 NT	3 ♥

NOTE, however, that if your major suit is *six* cards or longer, you should play the hand in your major suit. You know that you have at least an eight-card fit because partner would not have opened the bidding 1 Notrump without at least two cards in your suit.

Example: Responder holds
♠ 8 7
♥ K Q J 10 9 8
♦ A 5
♣ 8 7 6

Opener	Responder
1 NT	4 ♥

RESPONSES TO AN OPENING 2 NOTRUMP BID

When partner opens the bidding 2 Notrump, he shows a notrump-type hand with 22 to 24 high-card points. You may bid 3 ♣ as Stayman in response to partner's 2 Notrump opening bid. You may also bid 3 ◊, 3 ♡, or 3 ♠ any time you have a suit of at least five cards in diamonds, hearts, or spades. However, unlike your response to partner's 1 Notrump opening bid, these bids are not sign-offs. Rather, *any* response you make to a 2 Notrump opening bid is forcing to game.

After partner has opened the bidding with 2 Notrump, you should count your points and add them to partner's. This will give you the information needed to tell you whether to play the hand in game or slam. Occasionally, you will pass partner's 2 Notrump opening bid. You will do this when you have a hand with 0-2 high-card points. However, when you have three or more high-card points you should find a response.

RESPONSES TO AN OPENING 3 NOTRUMP BID

When partner opens the bidding with 3 Notrump, we know he has a notrump-type hand containing 25-27 high-card points. When partner opens with 3 Notrump, we obviously do not have to worry about whether the hand will be committed to game—it already is. Normally, you will pass partner's 3 Notrump opening bid. However, if you have eight or more high-card points, you will want to get to a slam. Remember, partner has at least 25 high-card points, so if you have eight points, there should be sufficient strength for slam.

Although you will normally be satisfied with a game contract when partner opens 3 Notrump, you may not want to play the hand in notrump. Consider the following example. You hold:

> ♠ Q J 9 8 7 4
> ♡ 5
> ◊ 6 5 3
> ♣ 5 4 2

If partner opens the bidding with 3 Notrump, you will respond 4♠ on this hand. Partner must have at least two-card support for your spade suit and spades will, in all likelihood, play much better than notrump.

Now test your knowledge of responses to opening notrump bids by answering the problems posed in Quiz No. 8.

QUIZ NO. 8

1. You hold	♠ 5 ♡ K 9 8 5 4 3 ◇ 3 2 ♣ 9 7 6 3	**Partner** 1 NT	**You** ?
2. You hold	♠ K 6 5 ♡ Q 5 4 ◇ Q 10 7 4 ♣ K 9 4	**Partner** 1 NT	**You** ?
3. You hold	♠ K 6 5 ♡ Q 5 4 ◇ 10 7 4 3 ♣ K 9 4	**Partner** 1 NT	**You** ?
4. You hold	♠ 6 5 4 ♡ Q 5 4 ◇ 10 7 4 3 ♣ K 9 4	**Partner** 1 NT	**You** ?
5. You hold	♠ Q 6 5 ♡ Q 5 4 2 ◇ Q 10 7 ♣ K 9 4	**Partner** 1 NT	**You** ?
6. You hold	♠ 9 6 5 ♡ Q 5 4 2 ◇ 10 7 4 ♣ K 9 4	**Partner** 1 NT	**You** ?

		Partner	You
7. You hold	♠ 9 6 5 ♡ Q 5 4 ◇ 10 7 4 2 ♣ 10 9 4	1 NT	?
8. You hold	♠ K J 9 7 6 3 ♡ 9 2 ◇ A J 3 ♣ 5 3	1 NT	?
9. You hold	♠ K 6 4 ♡ 8 6 4 ◇ 10 6 5 4 ♣ 9 7 4	2 NT	?
10. You hold	♠ K 6 4 3 ♡ 8 6 4 ◇ 10 6 5 ♣ 9 7 4	2 NT	?
11. You hold	♠ K 8 4 ♡ Q 10 4 ◇ A 7 6 5 ♣ Q 4 3	2 NT	?

ANSWERS TO QUIZ NO. 8

1. 2♡

2. 3 Notrump

3. 2 Notrump

4. Pass

5. 2♣

6. Pass

7. Pass

8. 4♠

9. 3 Notrump

10. 3♣

11. 6 Notrump

Chapter 9
OPENER'S REBIDS

To set the stage for this chapter, assume that you have opened the bidding and that your partner has responded to your opening bid. It is now your turn, as opener, to bid again, and your second bid is called *opener's rebid*.

THINK NOW—BID LATER

It is normally not too difficult to select your proper opening bid, nor is it difficult for responder to select his initial bid. However, before opener makes his rebid, he should stop to consider the information which is available to him. Sometimes opener will know a great deal about the hand, and very often will know exactly what the final contract should be. In those instances, opener need do nothing other than place the final contract by bidding it. On other occasions, the correct final contract will not be apparent. When that is the situation, opener should use his rebid to more fully describe his hand, thereby enabling responder to make an intelligent decision at his second turn to bid.

First, let's look at some of the judgment situations:

Example 1: You hold   ♠ Q 9 2
                  ♡ A K 5 4 3
                  ◊ A 4 3 2
                  ♣ 6

You (opener)	Responder
1 ♡	2 ♡
?	

Let's analyze this example. You have 13 points in high cards plus two points in distribution for the singleton club for a total of 15 points. Your partner's 2♡ response shows 6-9 points. Even if partner has the maximum nine points for his response, giving the partnership a total of 24, you know that you do not have the 26 points needed for game. You should therefore pass.

**DON'T FORGET
TO THINK
BEFORE YOU SPEAK.**

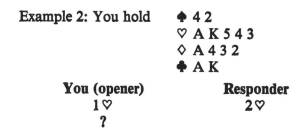

Example 2: You hold   ♠ 4 2
                        ♡ A K 5 4 3
                        ◊ A 4 3 2
                        ♣ A K

You (opener)	Responder
1♡	2♡
?	

On the above example, opener's rebid is 4♡. Opener adds his known 20 points to responder's known total of 6-9 points. Slam is out of the question, since a combined total of 33 points is required to bid and make a slam. Opener knows that the combined hands contain 26-29 points. His correct bid is 4♡.

Example 3: You hold   ♠ J 2
                        ♡ A K 5 4 3
                        ◊ A 4 3 2
                        ♣ A 5

You (opener)	Responder
1♡	2♡
?	

Clearly you cannot pass for the reason that responder may have nine points. If responder does, in fact, have nine points, then you want to be in game in hearts. However, if responder has only six points, you do not want to be in game. Opener's proper rebid is 3♡, passing the decision back to partner. Responder will pass 3♡ with only six or seven points for his 2♡ response, and will bid 4♡ if he has eight or nine points for his initial response.

Let's look at some more examples.

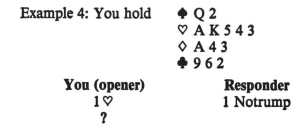

Example 4: You hold   ♠ Q 2
                        ♡ A K 5 4 3
                        ◊ A 4 3
                        ♣ 9 6 2

You (opener)	Responder
1♡	1 Notrump
?	

Your proper action is Pass. Partner has 6-9 points, and game is not possible.

Example 5: You hold

♠ Q 2
♡ A K 5 4 3
◇ A 4 3
♣ A K 2

You (opener)	Responder
1 ♡	1 Notrump
?	

Your proper action is 3 Notrump. The combined hands are known to contain 26-29 points.

Example 6: You hold

♠ Q 3 2
♡ A K 5 4 3
◇ A 4 3
♣ A 5

You (opener)	Responder
1 ♡	2 Notrump
?	

Your proper action is 3 Notrump. The combined hands are known to contain 30-32 high-card points, more than sufficient for game but not enough for slam.

WHAT IF PARTNER HASN'T TOLD YOU ENOUGH WITH HIS RESPONSE TO ENABLE YOU TO PLACE THE FINAL CONTRACT?

Many times partner's initial response does not tell you how many points he has within a narrow range. Consider this example. You hold:

♠ A J 5 2
♡ 4 2
◊ K 3 2
♣ A J 9 2

You	Partner
1♣	1♡
?	

Do you know what the final contract should be? Of course not. Responder has shown a hand containing at least six points with at least a four-card heart suit. If responder has only six points, you certainly cannot make game. However, responder may have 10, 12, or even 17 points for his 1♡ response. When partner makes a bid showing a hand that may contain enough points to make game, even if you have a minimum for your previous bidding, his bid is *forcing*. You are required to bid at least once more in order to give partner a chance to clarify his hand.

In the current example you have shown a minimum of 13 points by opening the bidding. Your partner's 1♡ bid has a range of six to 18 points. Since he *may* have the 13 or more points necessary for game, you must not pass 1♡. His bid is forcing.

If partner had instead responded 1 Notrump or 2♣ to your 1♣ opening bid, he would have limited his hand to a maximum of nine points. Consequently, a 1 Notrump or 2♣ response to your 1♣ opening bid would not be forcing.

Consider a further example. You hold:

♠ A K 5 4 2
♡ 9 2
◊ A 10 3
♣ Q J 2

You	Partner
1♠	2♣
?	

Do you know what the final contract should be? Again, you do not know, because partner may have anywhere from 10 to 18 points and has not had an opportunity to show you how many points he has within a narrow range.

When partner has responded in such a fashion that you cannot intelligently place the final contract, try to describe the strength of *your* hand within as narrow a range as possible. Partner will then use that information to accurately place the final contract. In this example, partner knows you have five spades because you opened the bidding 1♠. You should now show your club support by bidding 3♣.

MINIMUM REBIDS

You are fully aware that 13 points are required to open the bidding. When you are fortunate enough to be able to open the bidding, you will find that on the majority of occasions you will have a minimum opening bid; that is, a hand containing 13-15 points. Use the following procedure to describe such a hand:

A. First, check to see if you have four or more cards in partner's suit. If so, raise that suit to the next higher level.

Example: You hold   ♠ A 5 2
                  ♡ K 4 3 2
                  ◇ 9 2
                  ♣ A Q 10 8

Opener	Responder
1♣	1♡
?	

Your proper rebid on the above hand is 2♡. This tells partner that you have four-card support for hearts with 13-15 points. Partner will then be able to place the final contract.

B. If you do not have four-card support for partner but have a six-card suit of your own, rebid it at the lowest possible level.

Example: You hold   ♠ 9 5
                      ♡ 9 7
                      ◇ A K 6 4 3 2
                      ♣ A Q 8

Opener	Responder
1 ◇	1 ♡
?	

Your proper rebid is 2 ◇, showing a hand with fewer than four hearts, six or more diamonds, and 13-15 points.

C. Without four-card support for partner's suit or a six-card suit of your own, but with an unbid four-card suit, bid this suit if you can do so at the one level.

Example: You hold   ♠ K Q J 4
                      ♡ K 5
                      ◇ 8 7
                      ♣ A 9 8 5 3

Opener	Responder
1 ♣	1 ♡
?	

Your correct bid is 1 ♠.

D. Rebid 1 Notrump with a balanced hand.

Example: You hold   ♠ K 4 3
                      ♡ 7 5
                      ◇ A Q 7 2
                      ♣ A 9 5 4

Opener	Responder
1 ◇	1 ♡
?	

On the above hand, rebid 1 Notrump, describing a balanced hand with 13-15 points.

REBIDDING WITH 16-18 POINTS

A. With four-card support for partner's suit, jump raise his suit.

Example: You hold
- ♠ 9
- ♡ A Q 4 2
- ◊ K J 9 8 6
- ♣ A J 10

Opener	Responder
1 ◊	1 ♡
?	

Opener should bid 3 ♡ on the above hand, describing a hand containing 16-18 points with four-card support for partner's suit.

B. Jump rebid a six-card or longer suit of your own.

Example: You hold
- ♠ 9 2
- ♡ K J 2
- ◊ A K 10 7 6 2
- ♣ A J

Opener	Responder
1 ◊	1 ♠
?	

Your proper rebid on the above hand is 3 ◊, showing 16-18 points with a suit containing six or more cards.

C. With 16-18 points and a balanced hand, a rebid problem does not exist; you should have opened 1 Notrump in the first place.

Example: You hold
- ♠ A Q 3
- ♡ K 4 2
- ◊ A 10 6 3
- ♣ A J 4

If you open the bidding on this hand 1 ◊, you will have an extremely difficult time describing your hand with your rebid. This is because the opening bid of 1 ◊ is incorrect. Balanced hands containing 16-18 points are not described by opener's rebid; rather, they are described by the opening bid of 1 Notrump. If this is unclear, you should immediately review Chapter 5.

D. With 16-18 points, an unbalanced hand, and lacking both four-card support of partner's suit and a six-card suit of

JUMP BIDS

your own, bid a new four-card or longer suit.

Example: You hold
- ♠ A 10 2
- ♡ A K 9 4
- ◇ A J 8 4 3
- ♣ 6

Opener	Responder
1 ◇	1 ♠
?	

Your correct bid is 2 ♡, showing four hearts and a better-than-minimum hand.

REBIDS WITH 19-21 POINTS

A. With four-card support for responder's suit, raise responder to the four level if he responded one of a major.

Example: You hold
- ♠ A Q 8 6
- ♡ A 2
- ◇ A K 7 6 3
- ♣ Q 3

Opener	Responder
1 ◇	1 ♠
?	

Opener's proper rebid on this hand is 4 ♠, describing a hand with 19-21 points and four-card support for partner's suit.

B. With a balanced hand lacking four-card support for partner's major, jump rebid in notrump.

Example: You hold
- ♠ A J 2
- ♡ K 3
- ◇ A Q 4 2
- ♣ A J 9 8

Opener	Responder
1 ◇	1 ♡
?	

The proper rebid on this hand is 2 Notrump, showing a balanced hand containing 19-21 high-card points.

C. With 19-21 points, lacking support for partner and lacking notrump pattern, jump shift in a new suit.

Example: You hold   ♠ 9 5
                          ♡ A K J 10 6
                          ◊ A K J 2
                          ♣ K 8

Opener	Responder
1 ♡	1 ♠
?	

The proper rebid on this hand is 3 ◊, showing an unbalanced hand containing 19-21 points.

The alert reader may have noticed that you have now been supplied with a definitive method of showing all notrump-type hands within a three-point range. The following chart may be helpful in refreshing your memory:

HOW TO SHOW A NOTRUMP (BALANCED) HAND

13-15 points . . . . Open one of a suit and rebid cheapest notrump

16-18 points . . . . Open 1 Notrump

19-21 points . . . . Open one of a suit and jump rebid in notrump

22-24 points . . . . Open 2 Notrump

25-27 points . . . . Open 3 Notrump

You are also able to show most unbalanced hands with one or two bids. The following chart summarizes the bidding of unbalanced hands.

13-15 points . . . . Raise responder's suit with four-card support; without support, rebid a six-card or longer suit or bid a new four-card suit

16-18 points . . . . Jump raise partner's suit with four-card support; without support, jump rebid a suit of your own with six or more cards, or bid a new four-card suit

19-21 points . . . . Raise partner's suit to the four level with four-card support; jump shift in a new suit without support

22 or more points . . . . Open the bidding with two of your longest suit

Now test your knowledge of rebids by trying Quiz No. 9.

QUIZ NO. 9

1. You hold   ♠ 8 5   Opener: 1 ♡
                ♡ A K J 9 7   Responder: 2 ♡
                ◇ K Q 4   Opener's rebid: _____
                ♣ 10 7 2

2. You hold   ♠ 8 5   Opener: 1 ♡
                ♡ A K J 9 7   Responder: 1 ♠
                ◇ K Q 4   Opener's rebid: _____
                ♣ 10 7 2

3. You hold   ♠ 8 5   Opener: 1 ♡
                ♡ A K J 9 7   Responder: 1 Notrump
                ◇ K Q 4   Opener's rebid: _____
                ♣ 10 7 2

4. You hold   ♠ A Q 5 2   Opener: 1♣
             ♡ 9 2   Responder: 1♠
             ◊ K J 7   Opener's rebid: _____
             ♣ K 10 5 4

5. You hold   ♠ A 10 5 2   Opener: 1♣
             ♡ 9   Responder: 1♠
             ◊ K J 2   Opener's rebid: _____
             ♣ A K 5 3 2

6. You hold   ♠ A Q 5 2   Opener: 1♣
             ♡ A   Responder: 1♠
             ◊ K J 2   Opener's rebid: _____
             ♣ A Q 5 3 2

7. You hold   ♠ A J 4   Opener: 1◊
             ♡ 8 7   Responder: 1♡
             ◊ A K 5 2   Opener's rebid: _____
             ♣ A K 4 3

8. You hold   ♠ K 3   Opener: 1♡
             ♡ A K J 9 7 4   Responder: 1♠
             ◊ A J 2   Opener's rebid: _____
             ♣ 6 3

9. You hold   ♠ K 3   Opener: 1♡
             ♡ A K J 9 7 4   Responder: 2♣
             ◊ A J 2   Opener's rebid: _____
             ♣ 6 3

10. You hold   ♠ K 3   Opener: 1♡
             ♡ A K J 9 7 4   Responder: 2◊
             ◊ A J 2   Opener's rebid: _____
             ♣ 6 3

11. You hold   ♠ A K J 9 7   Opener: 1♠
             ♡ A K 4 2   Responder: 2♠
             ◊ A 5   Opener's rebid: _____
             ♣ 3 2

12. You hold   ♠ A K J 9 7   Opener: 1 ♠
                 ♡ A K 4 2   Responder: 1 Notrump
                 ◇ A 5   Opener's rebid: _____
                 ♣ 3 2

13. You hold   ♠ A K J 9 7   Opener: 1 ♠
                 ♡ A K 4 2   Responder: 2 ♣
                 ◇ A 5   Opener's rebid: _____
                 ♣ 3 2

ANSWERS TO QUIZ NO. 9

1. Pass

2. 1 Notrump

3. Pass

4. 2♠

5. 3♠

6. 4♠

7. 2 Notrump

8. 3♡

9. 3♡

10. 3♡

11. 4♠

12. 3♡

13. 3♡

Chapter 10
DOUBLES

In addition to the bids we have previously learned, there exists another bid called a *double*. When it is your turn to bid, you may, if the opponents have bid, double their bid in lieu of passing or making a bid in a suit of your own.

Doubles are primarily of two types: *penalty doubles* and *take-out doubles*.

A penalty double is a double of the opponents' final contract made with a view toward setting that contract.

Example:	Opponent	You	Opponent	Partner
	1 ♡	Pass	2 ♡	Pass
	4 ♡	Double	Pass	Pass
	Pass			

In the above auction, the final contract is 4 ♡ doubled. This means that if you set the opponents' contract, you will score more premium points than you would had you not doubled (see Chapter 2). Conversely, if the opponents make their doubled contract, they will score more points than they would have scored had there been no double.

Another type of double is called a *take-out double*. A take-out double is a double made at your first opportunity to bid and asks partner to bid his best suit. Further, for a double to qualify as a take-out double, partner cannot have bid anything during the auction other than pass. If partner has already bid a suit or notrump prior to your double, then your double will be for penalties rather than take-out.

REQUIREMENTS FOR A TAKE-OUT DOUBLE

In order to make a take-out double, your hand must meet *all* of the following requirements:

1. The strength to open the bidding (13 + points).
2. At least three cards in each of the unbid suits.

3. No more than two cards in the opponents' suit.

NOTE: The requirements outlined above for making a take-out double apply when the opponents have opened the bidding with one of a suit. However, these requirements do not apply when the opponents have opened the bidding one notrump. To double a one notrump opening bid requires a hand at least equal in strength to that of the opening bidder. In short, you must have at least 16 points to double an opening one notrump bid.

Example A: You hold   ♠ A J 9 3
                          ♡ K 9 7 5
                          ◊ A J 4 2
                          ♣ 8

If everyone remains silent, you will have no problem opening the bidding with 1 ◊. However, what if partner deals and the auction proceeds as follows:

Partner	RHO*	You
Pass	1 ♣	?

Here you have an ideal example of a take-out double. You should double, telling partner that you have an opening hand with support for all suits other than clubs.

Another example of a take-out double is shown below:

Example B: You hold   ♠ 6
                          ♡ A J 4 2
                          ◊ K Q 9 7
                          ♣ A 9 3 2

Your RHO opens the bidding 1 ♠. It is your turn to call. Again, you should double, announcing a hand containing at least 13 points and support for the unbid suits.

*The abbreviations RHO and LHO stand for right-hand opponent and left-hand opponent and will be used throughout this book when discussing opponents' bids.

Example C: You hold   ♠ K Q 3
♡ J 5
◊ A 7 6 5
♣ K J 9 8

RHO	You
1 ◊	?

Do *not* double. You have more than two diamonds and you also lack support for hearts. Your best course of action is to pass.

Another example of a take-out double arises when the following type of auction occurs:

LHO	Partner	RHO	You
1 ♡	Pass	2 ♡	?

Here, if you double, the double would be for take-out. You have not had an opportunity to bid and partner has bid nothing other than Pass. A typical hand for a take-out double in this situation is:

♠ K Q 10 4
♡ 9 2
◊ K J 7 5
♣ A J 10

RESPONSES TO TAKE-OUT DOUBLES

Assume partner has made a take-out double and your right-hand opponent passes. How do you respond to partner's double?

Before considering specific responses, we need to learn the general requirements for any response. Those requirements are as minimal as possible—0 points.

That's right! You should respond to partner's take-out double even if you hold no points whatsoever. Partner has not made a double for penalties and expects you to bid something no matter how weak your hand may be.

You should respond to partner's take-out double in the following manner:

A. With 0-9 points, bid your longest suit as cheaply as possible. If you have two suits of equal length—if they are a major and a minor—bid the major; if you have both majors, bid spades; if you have both minors, bid diamonds.

Example 1: You hold

♠ A Q 4 2
♡ 9 8 7
♦ J 7 6 2
♣ 9 2

LHO	Partner	RHO	You
1♡	Double	Pass	1♠

Example 2: You hold

♠ 9 2
♡ 8 7 4
♦ J 4 3 2
♣ 8 7 5 2

LHO	Partner	RHO	You
1♡	Double	Pass	2♦

B. With 10-12 points, jump the bidding one level in your longest suit. If you have two suits of equal length—if they are a major and a minor—bid the major; if you have both majors, bid spades; if you have both minors, bid diamonds.

Example 1: You hold

♠ A Q 7 6
♡ 9 2
♦ K 5 3
♣ Q 10 5 2

LHO	Partner	RHO	You
1♡	Double	Pass	2♠

Example 2: You hold

♠ 9 2
♡ A Q 3
♦ 9 8 6
♣ K J 10 9 2

LHO	Partner	RHO	You
1♠	Double	Pass	3♣

C. With 13 or more points in response to partner's take-out double, cue bid the opponent's suit.

Example 1: You hold   ♠ A Q 2
                              ♡ K J 4 3
                              ◇ K Q 3 2
                              ♣ 5 4

LHO	Partner	RHO	You
1♣	Double	Pass	2♣

Your cue bid says nothing about clubs; rather, it tells partner that you are holding at least 13 points in response to his take-out double.

Example 2: You hold   ♠ 3
                              ♡ A Q 4 2
                              ◇ K J 5 3
                              ♣ K Q 3 2

LHO	Partner	RHO	You
1♠	Double	Pass	2♠

Again, your call says nothing about the spade suit; rather, you are advising your partner that you have a strong hand.

RESPONDING TO PARTNER'S TAKE-OUT DOUBLE WITH A NOTRUMP BID

When partner makes a take-out double of the opponents' opening bid, he expects you to respond in your longest suit and show your strength as outlined above. Sometimes, however, it will be appropriate to respond 1, 2, or 3 Notrump.

The first requirement for responding in notrump to partner's take-out double is possession of a *stopper* in the opponents' suit. A stopper is a high card which will prevent the opponents' run of that suit. Normally if you have only one stopper in the opponents' suit, you should not respond in notrump, but should choose to bid another suit. However, with one or two stoppers in the opponents' suit, it is often right to respond in notrump to partner's take-out double.

A response of 1 Notrump to partner's take-out double shows 7-10 high-card points. A response of 2 Notrump shows 11-12 HCPs, and a response of 3 Notrump shows 13-15 HCPs. Each of these bids denies an unbid four-card major.

Example 1: You hold ♠ A Q 2
♡ J 5 4
◇ 10 7 2
♣ J 4 3 2

LHO	Partner	RHO	You
1 ♣	Double	Pass	1 Notrump

Example 2: You hold ♠ 9 5
♡ K 10 4 2
◇ A Q 5
♣ Q 10 9 6

LHO	Partner	RHO	You
1 ♡	Double	Pass	2 Notrump

Example 3: You hold ♠ K 4 2
♡ Q 10 9
◇ A J 10 3
♣ K J 3

LHO	Partner	RHO	You
1 ◇	Double	Pass	3 Notrump

Should you ever pass a take-out double? Yes, but only when you have at least five cards in the opponents' suit and four or more of the top six cards (A, K, Q, J, 10 and 9) in that suit. For example:

You hold ♠ A 5
♡ A Q 10 9 4
◇ 9 8 4
♣ 10 3 2

LHO	Partner	RHO	You
1 ♡	Double	Pass	Pass

With this hand, you certainly expect to defeat your opponents' contract of 1 ♡ doubled. When you pass your partner's take-out double, it asks him to lead a trump.

The accompanying chart summarizes the foregoing.

RESPONSES TO TAKE-OUT DOUBLES

SUIT RESPONSES

With 0-9 points . . . . bid your longest suit as cheaply as possible.

With 10-12 points . . . . jump the bidding one level in your best suit

With 13 + points . . . . cue bid the opponents' suit

NOTRUMP RESPONSES

With 7-10 HCPs and
stoppers in the opponents'
suit . . . . bid 1 Notrump

With 11-12 HCPs and
stoppers in the opponents'
suit . . . . bid 2 Notrump

With 13-15 HCPs and
stoppers in the opponents'
suit . . . . bid 3 Notrump

PASS
With five or more cards (including four or more of the top six cards) in the opponents' suit.

WHEN RHO INTERVENES

In the examples previously shown, after partner made a take-out double, your RHO passed. Sometimes your RHO will bid. When that happens, you are relieved of the obligation to respond to the take-out double with a truly bad hand.

Suppose you hold

♠ J 4 3 2
♡ 9 8
♢ 10 9 5 4
♣ Q 3 2

and the bidding proceeds

LHO	Partner	RHO	You
1 ♡	Double	Pass	?

You will respond 1 ♠, since you are obligated to bid, even though you have a very bad hand. However, assume that the auction has progressed as follows:

LHO	Partner	RHO	You
1 ♡	Double	1 ♠	?

Now you need not respond. You may pass, telling partner that you have a very bad hand and are not interested in entering the auction.

The outline of responses to partner's take-out double presented in the chart on page 117 is changed in only one respect by the fact that RHO has made a bid. When RHO bids a suit or notrump over partner's take-out double, you should pass with 0-5 points. With 6-9 points, you respond as you would have responded without a bid by your RHO. With 10-12 points, or 13 or more points, you bid exactly as previously outlined.

DOUBLING PREEMPTS

You will recall that an opening bid of 3♣, 3♢, 3♡, or 3♠ is preemptive, showing a weak hand with a long suit.

To double the preempt, partner should have a somewhat stronger hand than required for a take-out double of a one bid, since you will be forced to respond to the double at a higher level. An example of a suitable hand for a double of a 3♢ opening bid is:

♠ A Q 9 2
♡ K 10 3 2
♢ 3
♣ A K 5 4

Should partner double an opening preemptive bid, his bid is for take-out and you should respond in your longest suit, or bid 3 Notrump if you have the opponents' suit well stopped.

REDOUBLES

At this point, we introduce the only remaining bid in bridge of which you are unaware. That bid is called a *redouble*. You may redouble only when an opponent has doubled a previous bid. For example, the bidding proceeds:

LHO	Partner	RHO	You
1 ◊	Double	?	

Your RHO may bid a redouble at this point. (NOTE: The partner of the doubler can never redouble.)

You should use the redouble in two instances. The first instance is when your final contract has been doubled for penalties and you believe very strongly that you will make the contract.

For example:

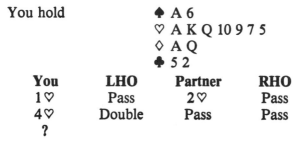

You hold

♠ A 6
♡ A K Q 10 9 7 5
◊ A Q
♣ 5 2

You	LHO	Partner	RHO
1 ♡	Pass	2 ♡	Pass
4 ♡	Double	Pass	Pass
?			

Here it seems a virtual certainty that you will make the 10 tricks required to fulfill your contract of 4♡. You should therefore redouble.

If the final contract is played redoubled (a highly unusual occurrence), the result is essentially to increase two-fold the doubled value of the contract. This increase applies both to premiums awarded should the contract be fulfilled and to points awarded to the defenders should they succeed in defeating the redoubled contract.

A far more common use of the redouble arises when you are responding to partner's opening bid and your RHO doubles. In this instance, your redouble tells partner that you have 10 or more points. No matter what your distribution, you should redouble with 10 or more points, and any other action by you shows less than 10 points.

Example: You hold ♠ A Q 2
♡ 9 7
◊ A 10 4 2
♣ 9 8 7 5

Partner	RHO	You
1 ♡	Double	?

You should redouble, telling partner that you have 10 or more points.

If you have less than 10 points and RHO doubles partner's opening suit bid, pass with 0-5 points. With 6-9 points, you should raise partner's suit with support for that suit. Without support for partner's suit and 6-9 points, bid your own suit as cheaply as possible.

REOPENING ACTIONS

Occasionally your LHO will open the bidding and both partner and RHO will pass. This leaves you the choice of passing, permitting the opponents to play a one level contract, or reopening the bidding.

You should reopen the bidding when you have 10 or more points. With 10-14 points, stoppers in the opponents' suit, and a balanced hand, bid 1 Notrump.

Example: You hold ♠ A Q 2
♡ 9 8 7 4
◊ K 3 2
♣ Q 10 2

LHO	Partner	RHO	You
1 ♠	Pass	Pass	?

You should reopen the bidding with a bid of 1 Notrump.

In the reopening seat, holding 10-14 points, you can simply bid a good suit of your own should you have one.

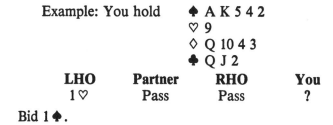

Example: You hold ♠ A K 5 4 2
                    ♡ 9
                    ◊ Q 10 4 3
                    ♣ Q J 2

LHO	Partner	RHO	You
1♡	Pass	Pass	?

Bid 1♠.

In the passout seat, make a take-out double (called a reopening double) when you have 15 + points or when you have 10 + points, three-card or longer support in each unbid suit, and no more than two cards in the opponent's suit.

The following quiz tests your doubling knowledge.

QUIZ NO. 10

For each example below, select the appropriate bid.

1. You hold ♠ 5 4 3 2
             ♡ A Q 4 2
             ◊ 9
             ♣ 10 8 5 3

LHO	Partner	RHO	You
1♠	Double	Pass	?

2. You hold ♠ 5 4 3 2
             ♡ J 9 7 5
             ◊ 9
             ♣ 10 8 5 3

LHO	Partner	RHO	You
1♠	Double	Pass	?

3. You hold
♠ K Q 10 7
♡ Q 5
♢ J 4 3 2
♣ J 10 2

LHO	Partner	RHO	You
1♠	Double	Pass	?

4. You hold
♠ K Q 10 7
♡ Q 5
♢ J 4 3 2
♣ K 10 2

LHO	Partner	RHO	You
1♠	Double	Pass	?

5. You hold
♠ 9 2
♡ 8 7
♢ A Q J 5 4
♣ A 10 9 2

LHO	Partner	RHO	You
1♠	Double	Pass	?

6. You hold
♠ A J 3 2
♡ 7
♢ Q 10 5 4
♣ A Q 10 2

LHO	Partner	RHO	You
Pass	Pass	1♡	?

7. You hold
♠ K Q 4 3
♡ A J 9 2
♢ 8 7
♣ K Q 10

LHO	Partner	RHO	You
1♢	Pass	2♢	?

8. You hold   ♠ K Q 9 7
                ♡ 2
                ◊ K J 7 6
                ♣ A J 4 2

LHO	Partner	RHO	You
1 ♡	Double	Pass	?

9. You hold   ♠ 10 5 4 2
                ♡ 9 8 7
                ◊ J 3 2
                ♣ 4 3 2

LHO	Partner	RHO	You
1 ♡	Double	Pass	?

10. You hold   ♠ A 5 4
                ♡ K 3 2
                ◊ A J 4 3
                ♣ 9 8 7

LHO	Partner	RHO	You
Pass	1 ♣	Double	?

ANSWERS TO QUIZ NO. 10

1. 2 ♡

2. 2 ♡

3. 1 Notrump

4. 2 Notrump

5. 3 ◊

6. Double

7. Double

8. 2 ♡

9. 1 ♠

10. Redouble

Chapter 11
OVERCALLS

An *overcall* is a bid made after the opponents have already opened the bidding. Sometimes your hand will not be suitable for a take-out double (not enough points or wrong pattern) or you may have a good suit of your own that you wish to bid.

The requirements for an overcall are that you have a suit of at least five cards and 10 or more high-card points. However, these requirements are not rigid—you must apply judgment in determining whether or not an overcall is justified. For example, assume you hold the following:

♠ 10 9 5 4 3
♡ A 2
◇ A Q 5
♣ 8 7 4

RHO opens the bidding 1 ♡. Should you overcall 1 ♠ on this hand? No. While you do have 10 points and a five-card suit, the suit is too weak for an overcall. One of the chief advantages of overcalling is to direct your partner to the best lead should the opponents ultimately play the final contract. In deciding whether to overcall, you should ask yourself this question:

If the opponents play the hand, will I want my partner to lead the suit I bid?

In the above example, the answer to that question is clearly no.

Now consider the next example:

♠ K Q 10 4 2
♡ 9 8
◇ A 10 5 3
♣ 8 4

RHO opens the bidding 1 ♡. You?

Here you have only nine high-card points, but this hand represents a fine 1 ♠ overcall. If partner has a reasonable hand with support for spades, you may be able to outbid the opponents. If not, and the opponents get the contract, you would certainly like a spade lead from partner.

Overcalls normally promise 10-17 points. With more than 17 points, you should not overcall because your partner may pass the overcall when the combined assets held by you and him are sufficient to make game. With 18 or more points, you should make a take-out double even if your pattern for making that double is less than ideal. If you overcall with a very strong hand (18+ points) partner may pass, resulting in a missed game or slam. This exception is the only exception to the rules for making a take-out double recited in the previous chapter. An example of a hand with which you should make a take-out double rather than overcall is shown below:

You hold   ♠ A K J 9 4
              ♡ A 2
              ◇ A Q 5 4
              ♣ 9 7

RHO	You
1 ♡	?

On this hand, you should double rather than overcall 1 ♠. It is true that you do not have support for clubs, but if partner responds 2 ♣, you will bid 2 ♠ anyway. This auction will tell partner that your hand is too strong for an overcall and that you hold a good spade suit. Partner will then be able to make an intelligent decision as to what to bid at his next turn.

1 NOTRUMP OVERCALL

An overcall of 1 Notrump shows the same number of points as does an opening bid of 1 Notrump. However, in addition to the 16-18 high-card points required for the bid, you should also have at least one stopper in the opponents' suit.

An example of a good hand with which to make a 1 Notrump overcall is shown below:

You hold   ♠ A J 4
          ♡ K 9 8
          ◊ A Q 10 2
          ♣ K 9 8

RHO	You
1 ♠	1 Notrump

In responding to partner's 1 Notrump overcall, I suggest that you ignore your opponent's opening bid and use the responses outlined in Chapter 8 exactly as if the opponents had passed and partner had opened the bidding 1 Notrump. This method has the advantage of being easy to remember and will normally land you in the right contract.

HOW DO I RESPOND WHEN PARTNER OVERCALLS IN A SUIT?

We know that when partner makes an overcall in a suit, he has a hand with 10-17 points and a suit of five or more cards. Since partner should not have more than 17 points when he overcalls, you should normally pass partner's overcall with a hand containing 0-7 points. With eight or more points, you should bid a good five-card or longer suit of your own, notrump, or raise partner's suit.

When you have eight or more points in response to partner's overcall, you should give first priority to raising partner's suit, if you have three-card or longer support for that suit. With 8-10 points, you should raise partner's suit one level. With 11-13 points, *jump raise* partner's suit; that is, raise partner's suit two levels. With 14 or more points, you should cue bid the opponent's suit.

On those hands where you do not have support for partner's suit but you do have eight or more points, you should respond to partner's overcall by bidding a good five-card or longer suit of your own. If you do not have a good suit but are well-heeled in the opponent's suit, respond with a bid of 1, 2, or 3 Notrump. A 1 Notrump response shows 8-10 high-card points, a jump to 2 Notrump shows 11-13 high-card points, and a jump to 3 Notrump shows 14-16 high-card points. With 17 or more points in response to partner's overcall, you should cue bid the opponent's suit, even if you have a notrump hand with stoppers in the opponent's suit. You will be able to bid notrump on the next round of bidding.

The following chart summarizes responses to partner's overcall:

RESPONSES TO OVERCALLS

WITH SUPPORT	WITHOUT SUPPORT
A. 8-10 points—raise partner one level	A. Bid a good five-card or longer suit of your own with 8-12 points
B. 11-13 points—jump raise partner's suit	B. With stoppers in the opponents' suit, bid:
C. 14+ points—cue bid the opponents' suit	1. 1 Notrump with 8-10 high-card points
	2. 2 Notrump with 11-13 high-card points
	3. 3 Notrump with 14-16 high-card points
	4. 17+ points, cue bid the opponents' suit

JUMP OVERCALL—A CHOICE AT LAST!

Throughout this book you have been given hard and fast rules which govern your bids in most situations. However, jump overcalls may be played several different ways, all of which are acceptable, and you should select the jump overcall most suitable to your taste.

A *jump overcall* is defined as an overcall which skips a level of bidding. For example:

1.	RHO	You
	1♠	3♣

2.	RHO	You
	1♡	3♢

3.	RHO	You
	1♢	2♠

All of the foregoing examples depict a jump overcall.

Jump overcalls may, by prior partnership agreement, be played as weak, intermediate, or strong. The requirements for each type of jump overcall are explained below:

A. Weak jump overcall—requires at least a six-card suit of good quality and 6-11 points with most of your points in the suit.

Example: You hold   ♠ 9 2
                    ♡ A Q J 9 8 7
                    ♢ Q 5
                    ♣ 9 8 2

RHO	You
1♠	2♡

The purpose of this bid is to preempt the opponents while at the same time advising your partner that you do have a good suit even though you were dealt a bad hand.

B. Intermediate jump overcall—an intermediate jump overcall shows 15-18 points with a good suit of six or more cards.

Example: You hold   ♠ 5 4
                    ♡ A 2
                    ♢ K Q 3
                    ♣ A K 10 9 8 7

RHO	You
1♠	3♣

C. Strong jump overcall—a strong jump overcall is a jump overcall showing a very good suit and a very strong hand. One making a strong jump overcall should require very little from partner in order to make game.

Example: You hold
- ♠ 2
- ♡ A K Q 10 5 4
- ◊ A K 3
- ♣ K 4 2

RHO	You
1♠	3♡

You and your partner may play jump overcalls as strong, intermediate, or weak, as you choose. You should discuss jump overcalls with your partner before you begin play and agree on the type most suitable to your methods.

OVERCALLING WITH A CUE BID

Sometimes your opponents will open the bidding and you will have an extremely strong hand; that is, one with which you would have opened the bidding with a strong two bid had you been given the opportunity. You can show this hand by cue bidding your opponent's suit at your first opportunity to bid.

You hold
- ♠ A K J 10 5
- ♡ None
- ◊ A K
- ♣ A Q J 10 8 4

Your right-hand opponent opens the bidding 1♡. Your proper bid is 2♡. You have overcalled with a cue bid of your opponent's suit. This bid says nothing about hearts. Instead, it tells your partner that you have a very strong hand and are forcing him to keep bidding until game is reached. Partner should respond in his longest suit, or in notrump if he has the opponent's suit stopped. If you overcall with a direct cue bid, the partnership is committed to game and neither you nor your partner should pass until game is reached.

QUIZ NO. 11

For each example below, select the appropriate bid.

1. You hold
   - ♠ Q J 10 5 3
   - ♡ A 4
   - ◊ 9 8 7
   - ♣ K 3 2

RHO	You
1♡	?

2. You hold
   - ♠ 5 2
   - ♡ A 6
   - ◊ Q 10 4 2
   - ♣ A K J 10 8

RHO	You
1♡	?

3. You hold
   - ♠ 9 8 7 5 2
   - ♡ K 3
   - ◊ A K 5
   - ♣ 9 8 3

RHO	You
1♡	?

4. You hold
   - ♠ K 5 4
   - ♡ A Q 2
   - ◊ K 4 3
   - ♣ A J 9 6

RHO	You
1♡	?

5. You hold
   - ♠ Q 10 2
   - ♡ 9 8
   - ◊ A 9 4 2
   - ♣ J 7 3 2

LHO	Partner	RHO	You
1♡	1♠	Pass	?

6. You hold   ♠ Q 10 2
            ♡ 9 8
            ◇ A J 9 4
            ♣ J 7 3 2

LHO	Partner	RHO	You
1 ◇	1 ♡	Pass	?

7. You hold   ♠ 9 2
            ♡ Q 10 4 2
            ◇ A K 5 3
            ♣ Q 10 2

LHO	Partner	RHO	You
1 ◇	1 ♡	Pass	?

8. You hold   ♠ A Q 2
            ♡ 4 3
            ◇ A Q 10 8 5
            ♣ K 9 2

LHO	Partner	RHO	You
1 ◇	1 ♡	Pass	?

ANSWERS TO QUIZ NO. 11

1. 1♠

2. 2♣

3. Pass

4. 1 Notrump

5. 2♠

6. 1 Notrump

7. 3♡

8. 3 Notrump

Chapter 12
PLAY OF THE HAND

The bidding is now over. You and your partner have outbid your opponents and you are the declarer in your final contract. You are faced with the task of making enough tricks to fulfill the contract. In this chapter, we examine the various methods of winning tricks and will also discuss the proper approach to the play of the hand.

Let's assume that you are declaring a contract. When your partner lays down the dummy, you know that your objective is to win tricks. Tricks may be won with high cards such as Aces and Kings and may also be won with low cards after the high cards have been played. For example, assume that you hold the following cards in a suit:

Dummy	9 8 7
You	A K Q 5 4 3

The above suit will usually give the partnership six tricks. First you play the Ace. Both opponents must follow suit if they can. Since you and your partner started with nine cards in the suit, the opponents started with only four cards in the suit. If both opponents have followed suit when you played the Ace, they have already played two of their four cards in the suit. Therefore, they have only two cards in the suit remaining. When you play the King and the Queen, these two cards must be played by the opponents. Now the five, four, and three are the only cards left to play in the suit. Therefore, these cards are now high and will win three more tricks.

TRUMPING OR RUFFING

In playing a suit contract, some suit will be named trumps. If the opponents lead a card of any other suit and either you or the dummy have no more cards in that suit, but have available a trump, you may *trump* (sometimes called *ruff*) that trick, thereby securing that trick for your side. An example of trumping or ruffing is shown below:

WINNING TRICKS

Dummy
♠ 5 4 3 2
♡ 2
◇ A Q 5 3
♣ 9 8 4 2

You
♠ A K 7 6
♡ 10 8 4
◇ K 7 6
♣ K 7 5

Assume that you are in a contract of 2♠ and that your left-hand opponent leads the Ace of hearts. You will play the two of hearts from dummy and the four of hearts from your hand. Your left-hand opponent next leads the King of hearts and, having no hearts in dummy, you may trump it by playing a spade. This will secure the trick for your side.

PLANNING THE PLAY IN TRUMP CONTRACTS

The following chart will help you in forming a successful plan of play in suit contracts:

PLANNING THE PLAY IN SUIT CONTRACTS

When the dummy comes down, ask yourself the following questions:

1. How many tricks must I win in order to fulfill my contract?

2. How many tricks must I lose and do I have any way of disposing of those losers?

3. How many tricks can I win "off the top" with high cards such as Aces, Kings, and Queens?

4. Can I afford to draw trumps now or do I need the trumps to ruff cards in the other suits?

If you plan the play, asking yourself the questions set out in the foregoing chart, you will normally come up with a very reasonable line of attack for each hand. While you may not be successful in making every contract, you will at least approach the hand in a workmanlike manner instead of in the haphazard fashion employed by most beginning players.

PULLING TRUMPS

When you are the declarer in a contract where some suit is trumps, it often is the best policy to extract (sometimes called *draw* or *pull*) the opponents' trumps as soon as you are able to do so. You do this to prevent your opponents from being able to win tricks with small trumps by ruffing in when you are playing high cards in the other suits.

The following example illustrates the devastating effect of failing to timely draw trumps:

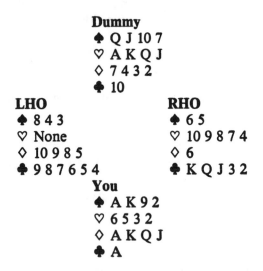

Dummy
♠ Q J 10 7
♡ A K Q J
♢ 7 4 3 2
♣ 10

LHO
♠ 8 4 3
♡ None
♢ 10 9 8 5
♣ 9 8 7 6 5 4

RHO
♠ 6 5
♡ 10 9 8 7 4
♢ 6
♣ K Q J 3 2

You
♠ A K 9 2
♡ 6 5 3 2
♢ A K Q J
♣ A

Assume that the contract on the above hand is 7♠. LHO leads the ten of diamonds which you win in your hand. It is now your lead. If you immediately play three rounds of trumps, extracting all of the opponents' trumps, you can then play your Ace, King, Queen, and Jack of hearts, followed by all the diamonds and the Ace of clubs. This will give you four tricks in spades, four tricks in hearts, four tricks in diamonds, and one

trick in clubs, for a total of 13 tricks. Thus, you will make your
7♠ contract. However, observe what happens if you fail to
draw trumps after winning the first diamond lead. Assume that
you attempt to play even one round of hearts before drawing
trumps. If you lead a small heart toward the dummy before extracting trumps, your LHO will ruff in with a small spade. He
will then lead a diamond which will be trumped by his partner.
His partner will return a heart which your LHO will trump.
LHO will lead another diamond which your RHO will trump.
Your RHO will lead a third heart which your LHO will trump.
Your opponents will have five tricks with their small trumps and
a contract of 7♠, which you should have made with ease, will
have gone down five tricks.

SHOULD I ALWAYS DRAW TRUMPS?

The answer is no, and your advance planning at trick one
should tell you when to draw trumps and when not to draw
trumps. Consider the following example:

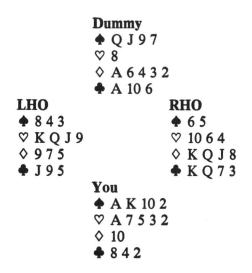

Dummy
♠ Q J 9 7
♡ 8
◇ A 6 4 3 2
♣ A 10 6

LHO
♠ 8 4 3
♡ K Q J 9
◇ 9 7 5
♣ J 9 5

RHO
♠ 6 5
♡ 10 6 4
◇ K Q J 8
♣ K Q 7 3

You
♠ A K 10 2
♡ A 7 5 3 2
◇ 10
♣ 8 4 2

The contract is 4♠. The opening lead is the King of hearts
which you win with the Ace. You can immediately draw trumps
as you did in the last example by playing three rounds of
trumps. If you do that, you will make the three rounds of
trumps you have drawn, the Ace of hearts, the Ace of

FOLLOWING SUIT

diamonds, the Ace of clubs, one heart ruff in dummy, and one diamond ruff in your hand. This will give you a total of eight tricks. However, you need ten for your contract. Is there a better plan?

You may observe that there is, indeed, a far superior plan. After winning the Ace of hearts you should, instead of drawing trumps, play a second heart and trump it in dummy. You should then play the Ace of diamonds, followed by the lead of a small diamond which you will trump in your hand. You should then play another heart and trump it in dummy followed by another diamond trumped in your hand. Next cash the Ace of clubs before your opponents have a chance to throw away all their clubs and follow this with a diamond from dummy ruffed with the King of spades. Then ruff another heart with the Jack of spades, the last diamond with the Ace of spades, and the last heart with the Queen of spades. There will be nothing left other than two small clubs in each hand and you will take 11 tricks instead of only eight tricks.

The principle to be derived from the foregoing example is that it is often correct to delay drawing trumps if you have cards which you need to ruff. Play out the hand above several times before going on.

THE FINESSE

A *finesse* is an attempt to win an extra trick or tricks for your side based upon the favorable location of the opponents' cards. The most common example of a finesse is shown below:

<pre>
                    Dummy
                    ♡ 8 4
        LHO   RHO
        ♡ 9 2   ♡ K 6
                    You
                    ♡ A Q
</pre>

Assume that the lead is in dummy and you lead the four. It is your right-hand opponent's turn to play. If he plays the King you will play your Ace. However, if your RHO plays low, you can play the Queen, and as your LHO has only small cards in the suit he can't win your Queen with the King. Thus you win two tricks in the suit: one with the Ace and another with the Queen, even though the opponents have a card higher than the Queen in their possession.

This type of play can also be repeated:

<pre>
                    Dummy
                    ◊ 4 3 2
     LHO   RHO
     ◊ 9 8 5   ◊ K 7 6
                    You
                    ◊ A Q J
</pre>

The lead is in dummy and you lead the two of diamonds. RHO plays the six of diamonds and you play the Jack which wins the trick. Rather than lead the Ace from your hand, you should now arrange to lead some other suit and take the next trick in dummy. When you arrive in the dummy, you can then lead the three of diamonds and once again finesse against the King held by your RHO. In this way, you can win three tricks in diamonds, never losing to the enemy King.

"But what if LHO holds the King?", you protest.

The answer to that is that LHO may well hold the King and will, in fact, do so 50% of the time. However, if you play the Ace without trying the finesse, you give up nearly all hope of avoiding the loss of a trick to the King. By finessing, you give yourself a 50% chance to win; without the finesse your chance is virtually zero.

OTHER SIMPLE FINESSES

You can finesse against other cards besides the King. For example, consider the following combination:

<pre>
                    Dummy
                    A K J
     LHO   RHO
     ? ? ?   ? ? ?
                    You
                    5 3 2
</pre>

If possible, you should first play the Ace to guard against the minute possibility that the Queen is a singleton. You should then return to your hand and lead toward dummy. If LHO plays small, play the Jack. If LHO has the Queen, you will have successfully finessed against the Queen and won this trick. However, if RHO has the Queen, you will lose the trick. Once again, it is much better to take the finesse, giving yourself a 50% chance, than it is to play the King, which virtually guarantees the loss of a trick to the Queen.

THE DOUBLE FINESSE

How many tricks can you win with the following card combination?

```
                Dummy
                A Q 10
      LHO                  RHO
      ? ? ?                ? ? ?
                You
                4 3 2
```

If you answered that you do not know, then you answered correctly. You know that the Ace will win at least one trick but you have no idea as to where the King and Jack are located. Let's examine this combination more closely in order to see how many tricks might be won in the suit depending upon the location of the opponents' cards. First, let's give LHO both the King and Jack:

```
                Dummy
                A Q 10
      LHO                  RHO
      K J 5                9 8 7 6
                You
                4 3 2
```

Proper technique with this combination is to lead a low card toward the dummy. If LHO plays low, you play the 10, winning the trick. You then return to your hand and lead toward the Ace-Queen. If LHO has both the King and Jack, as in this example, you will win three tricks with this combination.

However, what if RHO has both the King and Jack?

Dummy
A Q 10

LHO　　　　　　　　**RHO**
9 8 7 5　　　　　　　K J 6

You
4 3 2

Once again, not knowing the location of the enemy cards, you lead a low card and play the 10 when LHO plays low. RHO will play the Jack, winning the trick. When you next gain the lead, you will lead toward the Ace-Queen and play the Queen when LHO again plays low. Since RHO has both the King and Jack, he will win your Queen with his King and you will win one trick in this suit instead of the three you won when LHO had the King and Jack.

Finally, if the honors are divided:

Dummy
A Q 10

LHO　　　　　　　　**RHO**
K 5 3　　　　　　　　J 9 6 4

You
8 7 2

You lead low toward the dummy and when LHO plays low, you play the 10. RHO has the Jack and wins the trick. When you next regain the lead, you lead toward the Ace-Queen, playing the Queen when LHO plays low. This wins the trick. In this case, you win two tricks in the suit.

The previous examples graphically depict the power of the finesse and the importance of the location of the opponents' cards. Holding precisely the same card combination and playing in the correct manner, you saw that it was possible to win one, two, or three tricks. The result depended on which opponent held the missing honors.

Another common example of a double finesse is illustrated by the following card combination:

```
              Dummy
              A J 10
    LHO                  RHO
    ? ? ?                ? ? ?
              You
              7 6 5
```

How many tricks will be won in this suit?

Again, the answer is that you do not know. You will first play a low card toward dummy and if LHO plays low, you will play the 10. If this loses to the King or Queen, you will, upon regaining the lead, lead toward the Ace-Jack, and take a second finesse. If LHO has *either* or *both* honors (the King and Queen), you will win two tricks with this card combination. Note that the play of the Ace gives up virtually all hope of winning more than one trick with this combination. It is clearly superior to take two finesses.

PLAY OF THE HAND AT NOTRUMP

When playing a notrump contract, the declarer faces a job distinctly different from playing the hand in a suit contract. First, there is no trump suit, so you do not have to worry about drawing trumps. However, the disadvantage of not having a trump suit is that you cannot stop the running of an opponent's long suit by ruffing or trumping.

As in the play of the hand at a suit contract, you should formulate a plan at trick one and attempt to carry out that plan throughout the play of the hand. The following chart will assist you in developing a plan of play at notrump:

PLANNING THE PLAY IN NOTRUMP CONTRACTS

When the dummy comes down, ask yourself the following questions:

1. How many tricks must I win in order to fulfill my contract?
2. How many tricks can I win "off the top" with high cards such as Aces, Kings, and Queens?
3. What suit or suits can I develop to provide additional tricks needed to make the contract?

It is also important to develop the tricks you need in the suits to be developed before taking your Aces and Kings in the other suits.

Try the following hand to see if you are able to make your contract:

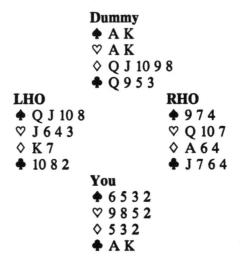

Dummy
♠ A K
♡ A K
♦ Q J 10 9 8
♣ Q 9 5 3

LHO
♠ Q J 10 8
♡ J 6 4 3
♦ K 7
♣ 10 8 2

RHO
♠ 9 7 4
♡ Q 10 7
♦ A 6 4
♣ J 7 6 4

You
♠ 6 5 3 2
♡ 9 8 5 2
♦ 5 3 2
♣ A K

Contract is 3 Notrump. Opening lead is the Queen of spades. Assume that you are the declarer in a contract of 3 Notrump on the cards shown above. Following the rules outlined for play of the hand, you first determine that nine tricks are required in order to make 3 Notrump. You next ascertain that you can cash the Ace-King-Queen of clubs, the Ace-King of hearts, and the Ace-King of spades, which will give you seven tricks. You therefore need two other tricks if you are to make your contract.

What is the most likely source of tricks in the above hand? Obviously these tricks can come from the diamond suit. If you can force out the King and Ace of diamonds, you will be able to win three diamond tricks.

How should you plan to play? You could immediately cash your Ace-King of spades, Ace-King of hearts, Ace-King-Queen of clubs, and then lead a diamond. If you do, you will go down miserably. Your opponents will take the remaining tricks in spades, hearts, and clubs and you will not be able to stop them from cashing their Queens and Jacks since nothing is trumps. Therefore, that play cannot work and you need to adopt an alternative plan. What plan is that?

As is most often the case in a notrump contract, you should *not* cash your Aces and Kings prior to setting up your long side suit, in this case diamonds. After winning the King (or Ace) of spades at Trick 1, you should lead a diamond. One of the opponents will win and will, in all likelihood, lead a second spade. You will win that trick and lead another diamond. The opponents will win that trick as well and will then be able to cash two more spades, bringing their total number of tricks to four. However, they will then have to lead one of the other suits, and you will be able to take three tricks in diamonds to go with the Aces and Kings you have in your three other suits, bringing your total number of tricks to nine and fulfilling your contract.

You should play over the preceding hand until you understand clearly how nine tricks can always be made at a contract of 3 Notrump with correct declarer play.

THE HOLD-UP PLAY

In declaring notrump contracts, you will often encounter suits in which you have only one stopper. If that is the case, it is often wise to *hold up*, refusing to release your stopper until you are forced to. A common example is shown following:

Dummy
♡ 8 4

LHO
♡ K Q J 10 2

RHO
♡ 6 5 3

You
♡ A 9 7

LHO leads the King of hearts. It would often be wise to refuse to win your Ace of hearts until the third round of the suit. Then, if RHO gains the lead later in the hand, he will be out of hearts due to your hold-up play, and might not be able to put his partner (LHO) on lead to take the two remaining hearts.

The reason for the hold-up play and its effect are shown in the typical example which follows:

Dummy
♠ A K 7 6 3
♡ 9 5
◊ J 5 4
♣ 8 6 2

LHO
♠ 10 8
♡ 7 4 3
◊ Q 8 7
♣ K Q J 10 9

RHO
♠ J 9 5 4 2
♡ A 6 2
◊ 10 3 2
♣ 4 3

You
♠ Q
♡ K Q J 10 8
◊ A K 9 6
♣ A 7 5

The bidding:

You	LHO	Dummy	RHO
1♡	Pass	1♠	Pass
3◊	Pass	3♠	Pass
3NT	Pass	Pass	Pass

The contract is 3 Notrump. The opening lead is the King of clubs. In the hand shown above, when the dummy comes down, you count your winners and see that you have the Ace-King of spades, the Ace-King of diamonds, and the Ace of clubs, which will give you five tricks off the top. You need four more and the obvious source of those tricks is the heart suit. If you can drive out the Ace of hearts, you can win four more heart tricks, bringing your total to nine tricks and enabling you to fulfill your contract. However, there is danger that the opponents may score five tricks before you are able to score nine. Observe what happens if you win the first trick with the Ace of clubs. You will then attack hearts, driving out the Ace. Your RHO will return his remaining club and your LHO will take four club tricks. Those club tricks, coupled with the Ace of hearts, give the opponents five tricks and you will go down one in your contract. However, watch what happens if you employ the hold-up play. You permit your LHO to win the first trick with the King of clubs. He then leads the Queen of clubs and you permit him to win again. He now leads the Jack of clubs and you win with your Ace. You lead the King of hearts and your RHO wins the Ace. He has no clubs and cannot put his partner in the lead to cash his two remaining clubs. You win whatever your RHO returns and are able to make at least four heart tricks, one club, two diamonds, and two spades, fulfilling your contract.

Play this hand several times, then turn your attention to Quiz No. 12.

QUIZ NO. 12

1. You should formulate a plan of play before playing to trick
_____.

2. When playing a suit contract, it is normally advisable to extract ("draw" or "pull") the opponents'
_____.

3. You should refrain from drawing trumps when you may need those trumps to _____ losing cards in other suits.

4. You hold   **Dummy**
                A Q
                You
                3 2

You lead the three, LHO plays low, you insert the Queen. Whether or not the Queen wins, the play you have executed is called a _____.

5. In playing notrump contracts, you should normally attempt to _____ tricks in your side suits before playing your _____ in other suits.

6. If you have only one stopper in the suit led by your opponents when playing notrump, what is normally your best course of action?

DON'T BE A BIDDING HOG

ANSWERS TO QUIZ NO. 12

1. One

2. trumps

3. ruff; trump

4. finesse

5. Establish or develop; high cards—i.e., Aces, Kings, Queens or Jacks

6. Employ the hold-up play

Chapter 13
DEFENDER'S PLAY

The bidding is over and the opponents are about to play the hand. Your RHO is declarer and it is your lead. What do you do?

Good defensive play is perhaps the most difficult aspect of bridge. When you play as declarer, you know as soon as the dummy goes down what the combined assets of both hands are and where the best source of tricks lies. However, as defender, you have no such advantage. Instead, you must apply logic and the information available to you from the bidding and the play in order to work out the best defense to enable you and your partner to garner sufficient tricks to defeat the contract.

One of the primary objectives of the defenders is to tell each other as much as possible about their hands and what they hold in each suit. This is accomplished by the order in which cards are played. Rules have been devised to cover a number of situations that commonly occur. We examine first the rules which apply to defender's play in both suit and notrump contracts:

A. TOP OF A SEQUENCE*

A *sequence* is defined as a holding of two or more cards in consecutive order of rank. Because you normally lead the top of an honor sequence, when you lead an honor you deny holding the honor directly above it. Thus, if you lead the Queen you deny holding the King. If you lead the Jack, you deny holding the Queen, and so on. When you lead from a sequence, you should lead the top card of that sequence.

Example 1:   K Q J — lead the King
Example 2:   Q J 10 — lead the Queen
Example 3:   J 10 9 — lead the Jack

---

*NOTE: "Standard" leading theory says that the appropriate lead from AKx is the King. An alternative, widely played and strongly recommended by this author, is to lead the Ace from this holding. This will avoid confusion between holdings in which you have the Ace, King versus holdings in which you have the King, Queen.

The effect of leading top of a sequence is illustrated by the example below:

Dummy
K 9 2

You   **Partner**
Q J 10 3   A 5 4

Declarer
8 7 6

Assume the suit in the example is spades and you decide to lead spades on this hand. Applying the rule of leading top of a sequence, you select the Queen as your opening lead. Declarer plays the King from dummy and your partner wins with the Ace. It is now your partner's lead. Your partner will return the suit which you have led and will know that you, rather than declarer, have the Jack, and that you should be able to win the next trick.

B. FOURTH BEST
When you do not have a sequence but have four or more cards in a suit you elect to lead, you should lead the fourth card from the top.

Example 1:   K 10 5 4 2 — lead the 4
Example 2:   Q 9 8 3 — lead the 3

C. LEAD LOW FROM THREE CARDS HEADED BY AN HONOR
When you decide to lead a suit containing three cards headed by an honor, you should lead your lowest card.

Example 1:   Q 9 3 — lead the 3
Example 2:   K 9 8 — lead the 8
Example 3:   J 7 2 — lead the 2

NOTE: It is normally ill-advised to underlead an Ace against a suit contract no matter how many cards you may have in that particular suit. However, it is perfectly acceptable to underlead an Ace when defending against a notrump contract.

D. TOP OF NOTHING

When leading from three small cards, you should lead the highest of those cards, and then follow with the second highest at your next opportunity. For example, with the 8-5-2, lead the eight, play the five next, and play the two last.

Example 1:   8 5 2 — lead the 8
Example 2:   7 3 2 — lead the 7

E. HIGH-LOW WITH A DOUBLETON

When you hold only two cards in a suit and elect to lead that suit, you should lead the higher of the two cards.

Example 1:   9 2 — lead the 9
Example 2:   8 6 — lead the 8
Example 3:   J 3 — lead the Jack

The foregoing methods of leading are designed to enable your partner to picture more clearly your holding in whatever suit you lead. However, those rules do not tell you which suit you should lead.

WHAT SUIT SHOULD I LEAD?

After a lifetime of playing bridge you will often find yourself ready to make the opening lead, ask yourself this question, and still not know the answer. However, there are general guidelines for selecting the best opening lead against suit contracts and against notrump contracts.

OPENING LEAD AGAINST NOTRUMP CONTRACTS

1. If partner has bid a suit, lead that suit.
2. If partner has not bid a suit, lead fourth-best in your longest suit. If you have two suits of equal length, lead from the stronger suit.

Example: You hold   ♠ Q 10 8 6 2
                     ♡ 8 4
                     ◇ J 3 2
                     ♣ Q 10 9

Let's assume that you are the opening leader with this hand and that your RHO is declarer in a contract of 3 Notrump. Let's assume that on the way to the 3 Notrump contract, your partner bid 1 ♡. That being the case, your proper opening lead is the eight of hearts.

Now let's assume that the contract is 3 Notrump and you hold the same hand; however, your partner has remained silent throughout the auction. That being the case, your proper lead is the six of spades.

The theory behind the two rules recited above is relatively simple. When defending a notrump contract, you want to develop your best suit as a source of defensive tricks as quickly as possible. It is logical to assume that if partner has bid a suit, that suit will provide a good source of tricks for your side. For this reason, you should lead it. On the other hand, if partner has not bid, you should look for a reasonable suit of your own which might provide a good source of tricks. On the hand shown above, if you are fortunate enough to find your partner with the King and Jack of spades, you may be able to make quite a number of spade tricks after you have forced declarer to play his Ace.

NOTE: Leading fourth-best against a notrump contract does not apply when you have a sequence or an *interior sequence*. When holding a sequence, you should still lead the top of the sequence, and when holding an interior sequence, you should lead the top card of the interior sequence.

Example 1:   Q J 10 5 4 — lead the Queen
(sequence)
Example 2:   K J 10 9 — lead the Jack
(interior sequence)
Example 3:   A Q J 10 2 — lead the Queen
(interior sequence)

WHY FOURTH-BEST?

You may wonder why you lead fourth-down from your longest and strongest suit against notrump. There is no particular reason for it other than that the lead of fourth-best has become accepted practice. However, if you and your partner employ these methods, you will be able to use another tool which can be very effective in defending. That tool is called the *Rule of Eleven.* The Rule of Eleven is a device which enables a defender to ascertain how many cards in a particular suit higher than the card led are held by the declarer. The mechanics of the Rule are that you, as partner of the opening leader, subtract the number of the spot card led by partner from eleven. For example, assume that the layout in the heart suit is as follows:

Dummy
J 8 6

Partner   **You**
?   A 7 2

Declarer
?

Assume that partner's opening lead is the five of hearts. To apply the Rule of Eleven, you subtract five from eleven, yielding a result of six. This tells you that there are six hearts higher than the five of hearts distributed among the dummy, your hand, and declarer's hand. Since you are looking at three cards in the dummy higher than the five of hearts and two cards in your hand higher than the five, you know that declarer has only one heart higher than the five. You should, therefore, immediately win the Ace and return a heart in an effort to set up your partner's suit.

Not much help? Sometimes you will be surprised at the information you can glean from the application of this rule. Look at another example:

Dummy
Q 8 4

Partner   **You**
?   A K 10

Declarer
?

Partner leads the six of spades. Declarer plays the four from dummy. Which card should you play?

If you applied the Rule of Eleven, you know that declarer

cannot have the Jack and that you may safely play the 10, winning the trick. Why? Partner led the six. Applying the Rule of Eleven, you subtract six from 11 which tells you that there are five cards higher than the six of spades distributed in some fashion among dummy, declarer, and you. Since two of those cards are in dummy and three are in your hand, declarer cannot have a spade in his hand higher than the six.

DEFENDING SUIT CONTRACTS

The principles which apply when defending suit contracts are somewhat different from the principles which apply when defending a notrump contract. In defending notrump, we normally want to establish a long suit so that we can win tricks with our low cards in that suit. However, this strategy will not work when defending a suit contract for the reason that after the suit has been played a couple of times, either the declarer or the dummy will be short in that suit and will trump it. We must, therefore, look for another strategy.

It is normally right to attempt to develop winners in suits where only one or two high cards are missing. For example, if you hold King-Queen-Jack in a suit, it would be correct to lead the King in an effort to force out the Ace and win subsequent tricks with the Queen and perhaps the Jack.

Another strategy that is often employed when defending against suit contracts is to try to win tricks with your trumps by ruffing. In an effort to do this, you will often lead a short suit and hope that partner can gain the lead and return that suit, enabling you to ruff. Look at the following layout:

<pre>
                    Dummy
                    ♠ A K 7
                    ♡ K J 9 7
                    ◇ K Q 8
                    ♣ Q J 9
You   Partner
♠ Q 10 8   ♠ 9 6 5 2
♡ 10 8 5   ♡ A 6
◇ 9   ◇ 10 7 6 3
♣ K 8 7 4 3 2   ♣ A 10 6
                    Declarer
                    ♠ J 4 3
                    ♡ Q 4 3 2
                    ◇ A J 5 4 2
                    ♣ 5
</pre>

The contract is 4♡. You elect to attempt a ruffing defense and therefore select as your opening lead the nine of diamonds. Declarer wins and immediately tries to draw trumps by leading a heart. Your partner wins his Ace of hearts and returns a diamond which you trump. You lead a club to partner's Ace and he returns yet another diamond for you to trump with your last heart. By this method of defense, you have procured four tricks, setting declarer's contract, when you would have been able to get only two tricks had you not led your singleton diamond.

OTHER DEFENSIVE STRATEGIES

A. SECOND HAND LOW

When you are the second person to play to a trick, it is usually correct to play low. The reason behind this strategy is that your partner has not yet played and will get to play last, hopefully beating whatever card the declarer has produced.

Example:

```
                    Dummy
                    A 9 5
     You                          Partner
     Q 8 3                        ?
                    Declarer
                    ?
```

Declarer leads a small heart toward the dummy. Which card should you play?
You should definitely play low. While it is true that declarer may hold the King-Jack-10 in his hand and play the nine from dummy, thereby winning the trick, you gain absolutely nothing by inserting your Queen. Instead, you should hope that if declarer plays the nine from dummy, your partner will be able to win this trick.

B. THIRD HAND HIGH

When you are defending a contract and are the third person to play, the situation is exactly the opposite of that described above. If you are the third hand to play, this means that your partner has led the first card to the trick and you must play as high as necessary to win the trick.

```
                    Dummy
                    A 9 5
     Partner                      You
     ?                            Q 8 2
                    Declarer
                    ?
```

Assume this is the layout in spades and your partner leads the three of spades. Declarer plays the five from dummy and it is your play. Which card should you play?
Here you should play the Queen. Partner may have the King and you will win the trick. On the other hand, partner may have the Jack and be able to win a trick after the King and Ace are forced out. Under no circumstances should you play a small spade in this situation.
Once again, this rule has other applications, but at this stage of your bridge development it will be good enough

for you to remember that in most instances it is correct to play "third hand high".

SIGNALLING

"What? You mean I can wave at partner or point to the suit I want him to lead in order to help us defend?"
No, we are not talking about those kinds of signals. In fact, as your bridge expertise develops, you will learn that the rules governing bridge strictly prohibit any type of mannerism or physical action of any nature which might suggest to partner a particular card to play or a particular suit to lead. On the other hand, there are many legal means of communication designed to assist partner in making the correct decision as to what to play next once he has gained the lead.

HIGH CARD ENCOURAGES

Partner leads a suit and you want him to lead it again. How do you convey this message? The answer is by playing the highest card that will not cost a trick in that suit. For example:

You hold   ♡ A 9 2

Partner leads the King, which is going to win the trick. You would obviously like partner to continue this suit and you therefore play the nine, which *encourages* partner to lead this suit again. Conversely, assume you hold the 9-5-2 of hearts. Once again partner leads the King. You have no help in hearts and would not like partner to lead that suit again. You therefore play the two of hearts which is *discouraging* and suggests to partner that a suit other than hearts should be led. REMEMBER: A high card encourages a continuation, while a low card discourages a continuation and asks partner to shift to another suit.

It is very important to note that attitude can be conveyed not only when partner has led a suit, but also when declarer is playing suits and you are discarding. For example, assume that the layout is as follows:

```
                    Dummy
                    ♠ 7 6 5
                    ♡ K Q 10 9
                    ◊ 7 6 3
                    ♣ A Q 9
You                                    Partner
♠ A Q 9 8 2                            ?
♡ 5
◊ Q 5 4
♣ 10 8 3 2
                    Declarer
                    ?
```

Assume that declarer is playing in a contract of 4 ♡. You lead a club, won by declarer. Declarer then plays the Ace of hearts followed by the King of hearts. What card should you discard?

The answer is that you should play the nine of spades. Why the nine? Because the nine tells partner your attitude toward spades is good. It tells him that you would like him to lead a spade when he gains the lead.

SIGNALLING A DOUBLETON TO OBTAIN RUFFS

You will recall from an earlier discussion that the play of high-low normally shows two cards in a suit. You can employ this signalling device to obtain ruffs on many occasions. For example, assume that you hold only the eight and two of spades and your partner's first two leads are the two highest spades. Assuming that declarer is playing in a heart, diamond, or club contract, you may obtain a spade ruff by playing the eight followed by the two, encouraging partner to lead a third round of spades which you will trump. Partner should continue the suit, giving you a spade ruff.

Now test your defensive knowledge by answering the questions in Quiz No. 13.

QUIZ NO. 13

1. A holding such as K-Q-J is called a _____.
   Should you elect to lead from a suit containing such a
   holding, the proper card to lead is the _____.

2. You hold K-5-2 and elect to lead that suit. The proper card
   to lead is the _____.

3. You hold 7-4-3 and elect to lead a card from that suit. Your
   proper lead is the _____.

4. High-low encourages a _____, often showing a _____ in that suit.

5. In leading against a notrump contract, assuming your partner has not bid, it is normally advisable to lead
   _____.

6. If partner leads a high card in a suit and you would like partner to lead that suit again, you should play the
   _____ card which will not cost a trick.

7. If partner leads a high card in a suit and you do not want
   partner to lead that suit again, you should play the
   _____ card you hold in that suit.

8. When declarer or dummy leads a card, the defender who is
   second in hand to play should normally play
   _____.

9. When partner leads a card through dummy or declarer and
   you are third in hand to play, you should normally play
   _____.

ANSWERS TO QUIZ NO. 13

1. Sequence, King

2. 2

3. 7

4. Continuation; doubleton

5. Fourth down from longest and strongest suit.

6. Highest

7. Lowest

8. Low

9. High

Chapter 14
SLAM BIDDING

You will recall from Chapter 6 that you and your partner will require about 33 points in the combined hands to make a small slam and about 37 points to make a grand slam. In this chapter, we will look further into slam bidding.

Any time that you are able to ascertain from your partner's bidding that his total points added to yours are in the range required for slam, you will wish to consider whether to go on or to stop at game. When you ascertain that sufficient points are present to search for slam, you should next begin to think in terms of *controls*.

Controls are defined as cards which will take the first or second round of any particular suit. Normally, first-round control is an Ace and second-round control is a King. However, if you are playing a suit contract, you have first-round control of a side suit if you are void in that suit. Similarly, you have second-round control of that suit if you hold only a singleton.

Sometimes you will want to explore for a slam and will be concerned about the number of controls which exist between your hand and partner's hand. Obviously, if you are missing two Aces, you will not want to bid slam. How are you to find out about the missing controls?

BLACKWOOD CONVENTION

A method has been devised to enable you or partner to inquire of each other as to the number of Aces and Kings in your hands. This slam bidding device, called the Blackwood Convention, was invented by Easley Blackwood many years ago. The convention is now popularly played throughout the world and is employed by nearly every successful bridge partnership.

The Blackwood Convention works like this:

At any time during the auction, either you or your partner may determine that sufficient points are present for slam and decide to explore to see if you have the necessary controls to undertake the slam. You are most concerned about Aces, and you may ask your partner how many Aces he has by bidding 4

Notrump. This bid says nothing about notrump. 4 Notrump is a question, and asks partner to respond to the question by telling you how many Aces he holds. Responses to the 4 Notrump Blackwood inquiry are as follows:

5♣ . . . . No Aces or all four Aces
5♢ . . . . One Ace
5♡ . . . . Two Aces
5♠ . . . . Three Aces

After partner tells you how many Aces he has in response to your 4 Notrump inquiry, you may either stop the bidding at the five level, bid six or seven of whatever contract you wish to play, or, if partner's response to 4 Notrump has indicated that the partnership holds all four Aces, you may then ask partner how many Kings he holds. You do this by bidding 5 Notrump.

After partner has responded to your 4 Notrump inquiry, 5 Notrump tells partner that you and he possess all the Aces, and asks him to show you how many Kings he holds. Responses to the 5 Notrump inquiry are as follows:

6♣ . . . . No Kings
6♢ . . . . One King
6♡ . . . . Two Kings
6♠ . . . . Three Kings
6 Notrump . . . . Four Kings

The following chart summarizes this information for you.

THE BLACKWOOD CONVENTION

4 Notrump...How many Aces do you have?
5 ♣.........No Aces or all four Aces
5 ♢ ....One Ace
5 ♡ ....Two Aces
5 ♠ ....Three Aces

5 Notrump...We have all the Aces. How
many Kings do you have?
6 ♣.....................No Kings
6 ♢ ....One King
6 ♡ ....Two Kings
6 ♠ ....Three Kings
6 Notrump ....Four Kings

In order to bid Blackwood, you should fulfill *all* of the following requirements:

1. You know that your partnership has 33 or more points.
2. You know the suit in which you want to play the final contract.
3. You believe that your partnership has first- or second-round control in each suit. This may occur because your partner has bid strongly or because you have a control in each suit in your hand. Do not bid Blackwood if you have two or more cards in an unbid suit unless you have the Ace or King in that suit.
4. You have no voids in your hand.

Examples:

1. Partner opens 1 ♠.

   You hold   ♠ K Q 8 6
                   ♡ 4
                   ♢ A K Q 8 4 3
                   ♣ A 5.
   Bid 4 Notrump (Blackwood).

2. You open 1 ♠ holding the following:

> ♠ A K Q 9 4 2
> ♡ 8 2
> ◊ K Q 7
> ♣ A 10

Partner bids 3 ♠. Do not bid Blackwood. If you do bid Blackwood and partner responds 5 ◊, you still won't know whether you can make slam. You may lose the first two heart tricks.*

WHAT IF PARTNER'S FIRST RESPONSE TELLS ME I CAN'T MAKE SLAM?

Occasionally you will launch the Blackwood Convention only to discover from partner's initial response that you cannot make slam. For example, suppose the bidding has gone as follows:

You	Partner
1 ♡	3 ♡
4 Notrump	5 ◊

Assume on the auction shown above that you hold only one Ace. Partner's response to your Blackwood inquiry also shows only one Ace and you know that you are missing two Aces. You should therefore bid 5 ♡, which your partner must pass.

CAN I STOP AT 5 NOTRUMP?

Yes, you can normally stop the bidding at 5 Notrump after you have initiated the Blackwood sequence. You do this by bidding an unbid suit at the five level after receiving partner's Blackwood response. This bid tells partner that you do not wish to go on to slam and want him to bid 5 Notrump. For example:

You	Partner
1 ♠	3 ◊
4 Notrump	5 ◊
5 ♡	

*If you would like to know more about correct slam bidding methods, a com prehensive book on the subject, *Blackwood On Slams,* is available.

Your last bid, a new suit at the five level, tells partner that you are not interested in slam and that you wish him to bid 5 Notrump. Partner will respond 5 Notrump and you will pass.

There are other methods of slam bidding, some of which employ other conventional bids and some of which do not. However, those methods are beyond the scope of a beginner's bridge book. Once you have gained considerable experience at bridge, you may wish to delve further into more advanced methods of slam bidding. Bon voyage!

QUIZ NO. 14

1. In order to bid a small slam, you and partner need about _____ points between the combined hands.

2. In order to bid a grand slam, you and partner need about _____ points between the combined hands.

3. Aces and Kings are sometimes called _____.

4. A response of 5 ◊ to a Blackwood 4 Notrump shows _____.

5. A response of 5 ♠ to a Blackwood 4 Notrump shows _____.

6. After partner has responded to your 4 Notrump inquiry, a bid of 5 Notrump asks partner for _____.

7. A response of 6 ♠ to 5 Notrump shows _____.

ANSWERS TO QUIZ NO. 14

1. 33 points

2. 37 points

3. controls

4. One Ace

5. Three Aces

6. Kings

7. Three Kings

GLOSSARY OF TERMS

above the line—All scores entered above the horizontal line on the score sheet, including penalties and other bonuses.

auction—Bidding by the four players for the contract.

balancing—Reopening with a bid or double when the opposing bidding has stopped at a low level.

below the line—All scores entered below the horizontal line on the score sheet; only those points for bidding and making part-scores or games.

bid—A call by a player in the auction.

Blackwood Convention—Bid to determine the number of aces and kings in partner's hand; initiated with a bid of four notrump.

book—For the declarer, the first six tricks taken.

call—Any bid, double, redouble, or pass.

cash—To play a winning card and win the trick.

contract—The undertaking by declarer's side to win a specified number of tricks; the final bid in any auction.

controls—Holdings that prevent the opponents' winning one or two immediate tricks in a specified suit; aces and kings, or voids and singletons in side suits at suit contracts.

cue bid—A bid in a suit in which the bidder cannot wish to play the contract.

deal—To distribute the cards to the four players.

declarer—The player who first bid the denomination of the final bid; the person who plays the hand.

defender—An opponent of the declarer; one who attempts to prevent the declarer from making his contract.

denomination—The suit or notrump specified in a bid.

discard—To play a card which is neither of the suit led nor of the trump suit; the card so played.

distributional points—Points added to the value of your hand for shortness in one or more suits.

double—A call that increases the scoring value of an opponent's bid.

doubleton—A holding of two cards in a suit.

down—Defeated; a declarer who has failed to make his contract.

drawing trumps—The action of removing the trumps from the opponents' hands.

dummy—Declarer's partner; dummy's cards are placed face up on the table and played by declarer.

establish—To make a suit or specific card good by forcing out the opponent's winner(s).

extra trick—Overtrick; a trick scored in excess of the number of tricks required to fulfill a contract.

finesse—An attempt to win an extra trick or tricks for your side based on the favorable location of your opponents' cards.

fulfilling the contract—Taking as many tricks in the play of hand as contracted for in addition to book; for example, nine tricks in a contract of three.

game—Contract of 3 Notrump, 4 Hearts, 4 Spades, 5 Clubs or 5 Diamonds; the winning of 100 points below the line.

go down—fail to make a contract.

grand slam—Bidding and winning all 13 tricks by the declarer.

hand—The 13 cards held by any player in a bridge game.

high-card points (HCPs)—Points assigned to aces, kings, queens and jacks.

hold-up play—Refusing to win a trick at the first opportunity.

holding—The cards a player is dealt in a particular suit.

honor—Ace, king, queen, jack or 10.

invitation—A bid which encourages the bidder's partner to continue to game or slam, but gives him the option of passing with minimum values.

jump overcall—An overcall which skips a level of bidding.

jump raise—A bid which raises partner's suit two levels of bidding.

LHO—Left-hand opponent.

lead—The first card played to a trick.

major suits—Spades and hearts.

minor suits—Diamonds and clubs.

notrump—The highest denomination in the bidding; contracts that are played without a trump suit.

notrump distribution—A balanced hand; one which contains no void or singleton; usually 4-3-3-3, 4-4-3-2, or 5-3-3-2.

non-vulnerable—A side that has not won a game in a rubber.

opening bid—The first call in the auction other than a pass.

opening lead—After the bidding has been concluded, the first lead made by declarer's LHO.

overtricks—Tricks won by the declaring side in excess of those required to make a particular contract.

part-score (or partial)—Any contract below game level.

penalty double—Double of the opponents' contract made with the intention of setting that contract.

preemptive bid—An opening bid at the three-level or higher, containing a long suit and limited high-card strength.

redouble—A call that multiplies the doubled penalty or bonus by two.

response—First bid by the partner of the opening bidder.

reverse—A rebid at the two-level or more, in a higher-ranking suit than that bid originally; for example; 1♣ - 1♠ - 2♡ or 1♡ - 2◊ - 2♠.

RHO—Right-hand opponent.

rubber—Unit of bridge scoring achieved by winning two out of three games.

ruff—Play a trump in a suit in which the player is void.

Rule of Eleven—Calculation to determine the number of cards in declarer's hand higher than the fourth-best lead made by partner.

sequence—Cards in consecutive order, such as K-Q-J or J-10-9.

set—The failure of a contract; to defeat a contract.

side suit—Any suit other than the trump suit.

sign-off bid—Bid intended to end the auction, requesting partner to pass.

singleton—A holding of only one card in a suit.

small slam—Bidding and winning 12 tricks by the declarer.

spot card—2, 3, 4, 5, 6, 7, 8, or 9 of any suit.

Stayman Convention—The response of 2 Clubs to 1 Notrump asking opener to bid a four-card major suit.

stopper—High card that will stop the opponents from running a suit.

takeout double—A double that asks partner to bid his best suit.

trick—Four cards comprise one trick, one card being played by each player; there are 13 tricks in every hand of bridge.

trump—The suit named in the final bid, other than notrump; to ruff.

void—A holding of no cards in a suit.

vulnerable—A side that has won a game in a rubber.

50 HIGHLY-RECOMMENDED TITLES

CALL TOLL FREE 1-800-274-2221
IN THE U.S. & CANADA TO ORDER ANY OF
THEM OR TO REQUEST OUR
FULL-COLOR 64 PAGE CATALOG OF
ALL BRIDGE BOOKS IN PRINT,
SUPPLIES AND GIFTS.

FOR BEGINNERS
#0300 Future Champions' Bridge Series 9.95
#2130 Kantar-Introduction to Declarer's Play 10.00
#2135 Kantar-Introduction to Defender's Play 10.00
#0101 Stewart-Baron-The Bridge Book 1 .... 9.95
#1121 Silverman-Elementary Bridge
      Five Card Major Student Text 4.95
#0660 Penick-Beginning Bridge Complete 9.95
#0661 Penick-Beginning Bridge Quizzes 6.95
#3230 Lampert-Fun Way to Serious Bridge 11.00

FOR ADVANCED PLAYERS
#2250 Reese-Master Play 5.95
#1420 Klinger-Modern Losing Trick Count 12.95
#2240 Love-Bridge Squeezes Complete 7.95
#0103 Stewart-Baron-The Bridge Book 3 .... 9.95
#0740 Woolsey-Matchpoints 14.95
#0741 Woolsey-Partnership Defense 12.95
#1702 Bergen-Competitive Auctions 11.95

BIDDING — 2 OVER 1 GAME FORCE
#4750 Bruno & Hardy-Two-Over-One Game Force:
      An Introduction 9.95
#1750 Hardy-Two-Over-One Game Force 16.95
#1790 Lawrence-Workbook on the Two Over One System 12.95
#4525 Lawrence-Bidding Quizzes Book 1 .... 13.95

Prices subject to change without notice.

DEFENSE
#0520 Blackwood-Complete Book of Opening Leads 17.95
#0104 Stewart-Baron-The Bridge Book 4 .... 7.95
#0631 Lawrence-Dynamic Defense 11.95
#1200 Woolsey-Modern Defensive Signalling 4.95

FOR INTERMEDIATE PLAYERS
#3015 Root-Commonsense Bidding 15.00
#0630 Lawrence-Card Combinations 12.95
#0102 Stewart-Baron-The Bridge Book 2 .... 9.95
#1122 Silverman-Intermediate Bridge Five
       Card Major Student Text 4.95
#0575 Lampert-The Fun Way to Advanced Bridge 11.95
#0633 Lawrence-How to Read Your Opponents' Cards 11.95
#3672 Truscott-Bid Better, Play Better 12.95
#1765 Lawrence-Judgment at Bridge 11.95

PLAY OF THE HAND
#2150 Kantar-Test your Bridge Play, Vol. 1 .... 10.00
#3675 Watson-Watson's Classic Book on
       the Play of the Hand 16.00
#1932 Mollo-Gardener-Card Play Technique 19.95
#3009 Root-How to Play a Bridge Hand 16.00
#1124 Silverman-Play of the Hand as
       Declarer and Defender 4.95
#2175 Truscott-Winning Declarer Play 10.00
#3803 Sydnor-Bridge Made Easy Book 3 .... 8.00

CONVENTIONS
#2115 Kantar-Bridge Conventions 10.00
#0610 Kearse-Bridge Conventions Complete 29.95
#3011 Root-Pavlicek-Modern Bridge Conventions 16.00
#0240 Championship Bridge Series (All 36) 25.95

DUPLICATE STRATEGY
#1600 Klinger-50 Winning Duplicate Tips 14.95
#2260 Sheinwold-Duplicate Bridge 6.95
#2800 Granovetter-Conventions at a Glance 8.95
#1750 Hardy-2 Over 1 Game Force 16.95
#2038 Seagram-25 Bridge Conventions You Should Know 15.95

FOR ALL PLAYERS
#3889 Darvas & de V. Hart-Right Through The Pack 14.95
#0790 Simon- Why You Lose at Bridge 11.95
#1928 Mollo- Bridge in the Menagerie 16.95

DEVYN PRESS INC.

3600 Chamberlain Lane, Suite 230, Louisville, KY 40241

1-800-274-2221

CALL TOLL FREE IN THE U.S. & CANADA
TO ORDER OR TO REQUEST OUR 64 PAGE
FULL COLOR CATALOG OF BRIDGE BOOKS,
SUPPLIES AND GIFTS.

Andersen THE LEBENSOHL CONVENTION COMPLETE .... $ 8.95
Baron THE BRIDGE PLAYER'S DICTIONARY $19.95
Bergen BETTER BIDDING WITH BERGEN,
 Vol. I, Uncontested Auctions $11.95
Bergen BETTER BIDDING WITH BERGEN,
 Vol. II, Competitive Auctions $11.95
Blackwood COMPLETE BOOK OF OPENING LEADS $17.95
Blackwood-Hanson PLAY FUNDAMENTALS .... $ 6.95
Boeder THINKING ABOUT IMPS $12.95
Bruno-Hardy 2 OVER 1 GAME FORCE: AN INTRODUCTION .... $ 9.95
Darvas & De V. Hart RIGHT THROUGH THE PACK $14.95
DeSerpa THE MEXICAN CONTRACT .... $ 5.95
Eber & Freeman HAVE I GOT A STORY FOR YOU .... $ 7.95
Feldheim FIVE CARD MAJOR BIDDING IN
 CONTRACT BRIDGE $12.95
Flannery THE FLANNERY 2 DIAMOND OPENING .... $ 7.95
Goldman WINNERS AND LOSERS AT THE
 BRIDGE TABLE .... $ 3.95
Groner DUPLICATE BRIDGE DIRECTION $14.95
Hardy
 COMPETITIVE BIDDING WITH 2-SUITED HANDS .... $ 9.95
 TWO-OVER-ONE GAME FORCE $16.95
 TWO-OVER-ONE GAME FORCE QUIZ BOOK $11.95
Harris BRIDGE DIRECTOR'S COMPANION (4th Edition) $24.95
Kay COMPLETE BOOK OF DUPLICATE BRIDGE $16.95
Kearse BRIDGE CONVENTIONS COMPLETE $29.95
Kelsey THE TRICKY GAME $11.95
Lampert THE FUN WAY TO ADVANCED BRIDGE $11.95
Lawrence
 CARD COMBINATIONS $12.95
 COMPLETE BOOK ON BALANCING $11.95
 COMPLETE BOOK ON OVERCALLS $11.95
 DYNAMIC DEFENSE $11.95
 HAND EVALUATION $11.95
 HOW TO READ YOUR OPPONENTS' CARDS $11.95
 JUDGMENT AT BRIDGE $11.95
 PARTNERSHIP UNDERSTANDINGS .... $ 5.95
 PLAY BRIDGE WITH MIKE LAWRENCE $11.95
 PLAY SWISS TEAMS WITH MIKE LAWRENCE .... $ 9.95
 WORKBOOK ON THE TWO OVER ONE SYSTEM $12.95

Lawrence & Hanson WINNING BRIDGE INTANGIBLES .... $ 4.95
Lipkin INVITATION TO ANNIHILATION .... $ 8.95
Michaels & Cohen 4-3-2-1 MANUAL .... $ 4.95
Penick BEGINNING BRIDGE COMPLETE .... $ 9.95
Penick BEGINNING BRIDGE QUIZZES .... $ 6.95
Robinson WASHINGTON STANDARD $24.95
Rosenkranz
    BRIDGE: THE BIDDER'S GAME $12.95
    TIPS FOR TOPS .... $ 9.95
    MORE TIPS FOR TOPS .... $ 9.95
    TRUMP LEADS .... $ 7.95
    OUR MAN GODFREY $10.95
Rosenkranz & Alder BID TO WIN, PLAY FOR PLEASURE .... $ 9.95
Rosenkranz & Truscott BIDDING ON TARGET $10.95
Silverman
    ELEMENTARY BRIDGE FIVE CARD MAJOR STUDENT TEXT .... $ 4.95
    INTERMEDIATE BRIDGE FIVE CARD MAJOR STUDENT TEXT .... $ 4.95
    ADVANCED & DUPLICATE BRIDGE STUDENT TEXT .... $ 4.95
    PLAY OF THE HAND AS DECLARER
      & DEFENDER STUDENT TEXT .... $ 4.95
Simon
    CUT FOR PARTNERS .... $ 9.95
    WHY YOU LOSE AT BRIDGE $11.95
Stewart & Baron
    THE BRIDGE BOOK, Vol. 1, Beginning .... $ 9.95
    THE BRIDGE BOOK, Vol. 2, Intermediate .... $ 9.95
    THE BRIDGE BOOK, Vol. 3, Advanced .... $ 9.95
    THE BRIDGE BOOK, Vol. 4, Defense .... $ 7.95
Truscott BID BETTER, PLAY BETTER $12.95
Von Elsner
    EVERYTHING'S JAKE WITH ME .... $ 5.95
    THE BEST OF JAKE WINKMAN .... $ 5.95
Wei PRECISION BIDDING SYSTEM .... $ 7.95
Woolsey
    MATCHPOINTS $14.95
    MODERN DEFENSIVE SIGNALLING .... $ 4.95
    PARTNERSHIP DEFENSE $12.95
World Bridge Federation APPEALS COMMITTEE DECISIONS
    from the 1994 NEC WORLD CHAMPIONSHIPS .... $ 9.95